AIRBNB BUSINESS, UPDATED EDITION

How to Start Your Highly Profitable & Fully
Automated Short-Term Rental Business.
Proven Methods & Latest Tips to Become a
Successful Superhost

STEVEN CARLSON

We invite you to scan this **QR code** using the camera of your phone to access your bonus content:

SCAN THE QR CODE BELOW

You will access to **2 EBOOKS**:

1. **"21 Productivity Ideas to Get More Done":** All the secrets to boost your productivity and achieve your goals effortlessly

2. **"Time Management For Entrepreneurs":** Everything you need to know to manage your time better so you can accomplish more and reach your goals

TABLE OF CONTENTS

INTRODUCTION

P eople primarily seek three things—food, clothes, and shelter. After the actualization of the first two essentials, the third becomes a sort of desire that becomes the means to build and sustain life. In our current day and age, owning real estate is a sign of status, wealth, and making a name. The utilization of real estate as a tool to generate cash flow or a source of investment can be dated back to when the first economies sprouted. Previously, barriers of entry existed for the mass populace to make use of their property for anything other than personal accommodation. Recent times have shown ample room for the barriers to tumble down. The crown for disrupting this territory can be given to the revolutions in real-estate investment and the short-term rental markets—with our focus on the short-term rental scene revolutionized by Airbnb. The company started on the precipice of the housing-market crisis of 2007–2008. In their blog, the founders reflect on the story of how they considered this radical idea of short-term homestays with random strangers. They tell the story of how back in 2007, two of the founders, Joe Gebbia and Brian Chesky, put up three inflated-mattress beds, and officially started the first Airbnb-stay experience. From then until now, the company has spiraled into a unicorn of the tech world and completely changed the hospitality industry.

This industry has grown into becoming the platform for individuals seeking the means to ditch their mundane work-life and set on the path towards financial independence. Browsing through various social-media platforms, one is bound to come across the stories of people boasting their success as an Airbnb host. As one should take everything they see on the internet with a grain of salt, hosting on Airbnb has time and again served to be an exceptional means of earning. This guide has been created to be the complete package for the potential host to provide top-tier value to their future guests. The opportunity has never been better and the room for growth has never been higher. Post-pandemic people all over the world are determined to make the most of the travel experience and accommodation at the heel of every trip. Airbnb offers the creative solution of disregarding the boring hotels and generic service and experiencing a dream stay in unique places with unique people. Hosting offers the means for individuals to effectively list their accommodations for the purposes of temporary arrangements.

The platform has been built to be a smooth and seamless onboarding for a potential host, and this guide has been built for the potential host to start their journey. Starting at listing your property, acquiring your first guest, managing queries, and getting your first earnings—everything has been carefully researched and laid out for you to absorb and begin. Allow us to help you be on the forefront of this creative nexus of staycation experience with hosting and travel. The world is seeing a resurgence of travel, and the timing could never be more perfect to consider this opportunity. From treetop houses to luxury towers, RVs, and caves, Airbnb has it all. No place is considered unworthy of being an Airbnb rental—if a niche can be targeted for those who might demand it. Hence, let us be your guide towards a life dedicated to serving your guests, managing your own properties, and creating a life of your own desires. If not now, when? If not us, who?

CHAPTER 1
AN AIRY SCENE

W̲e have all heard of Bed and Breakfasts (BnBs), which were quite the rage back in the day. BnBs can be dated back as far as 50 years. From times of festivities to crises, people have opened their doors to others for temporary, overnight stays. Soon the concept boomed worldwide, and more and more homeowners considered hosting as a means of earning something extra on the side. Since their inception, BnBs provided the guests a personalized experience of living rather than the often-dull walls of a hotel room. The experience was unique as it usually involved the guests staying the night at someone else's home—either in a different lodging or under the same roof in a separate room. The stay would be personalized with activities that permitted the locale of the neighborhood and its hosts. Satisfied customers would go on to state their experience as wholesome and unique as they were immersed in a stay that involved staying with strangers. In the process, moving from strangers to acquaintances and even friends. Moreso, allowing the guests to experience the hosts' culture, practices, and perceptions in a short and bearable period, which really added to the charm of the overall stay.

The Airbnb, at its core, is a platform that connects owners (hosts) to allow them to rent out a segment, room, or entire house/apartment to renters (guests) seeking short-term or even long-term stays. The company that started at the helm of the financial crisis of 2008 built its empire on the short-term tourist rental market. The business model adopted followed a collaborative practice which instilled a sense of camaraderie between the hosts, Airbnb, and the guests. The disruptive model aimed towards the hospitality industry offered the unique selling point (USP) of a local, staycation experience—a word play on a vacation accommodation which incorporated the personalized attributes of its locality. Instead of booking a room in hotels or resorts, guests would be able to access easy, affordable, and adventurous stays via the Airbnb platform. The business model allowed the natives of the area a passive source of income by renting out spare rooms or segments of their homes for temporary stay. Compared to traditional BnBs that required hosts to spend on advertising, the Airbnb platform took over the responsibility of branding and advertising. The hosts simply need to publish their listings based on their own preference—via pictures, description, rules of stay, and expectations. Additionally, the platform even takes the stifling responsibility of handling payments while giving comfort to the hosts by allowing them to set their rates. As the platform grew to incorporate over 500 million users, 7 million listings, and about 50,000 overnight stays per day, hosts and guests were able to access a myriad of listings and customers through a single platform; essentially, the ultimate advertising source for rental-unit owners (Serrano et al., 2020).

The business model of Airbnb is built around the peer-to-peer collaborative paradigm (i.e., the sharing economy.) The business essentially rents out and manages payments of properties it never actually owns. Like other booming peer-to-peer platforms, such as Etsy, Uber, or GrubHub, Airbnb banks on the service fees from both the hosts and the guests for operating through their platform. A reservation made on the platform provides a simple cost that the guest must pay; one part of the service fees that goes into Airbnb's pockets. Similarly, hosts are charged per the total earned income from any overnight stay at their listings. The rates for guests stand at 14% approximately, and for hosts, 3% of the total paid for the stay (Folger, 2022).

The Preference for Airbnbs

The company's statements are lodged at creating a space for an immersive experience of culture for its guests. "Belong anywhere" is the value Airbnb has portrayed to the world and its stakeholders. The mission statement speaks of the ability to *belong* as it enables its guests to stay in a new place instead of just visiting momentarily. At the heel of this ability lies the hosts who opened their homes up as a compromise. The hosts are the means of experiencing culture via the tool that is the Airbnb platform. The reasons for individuals choosing Airbnbs from other alternatives are a handful, and below, we list a few of the reasons behind it:

Local feel

The bedrock of this model is in providing a means for experiencing a distinct form of travel or vacation stay. Usually, guests seeking to travel to a new area wish to try or get to know the locality—its customs, practices, food, art, and lifestyle. Given the fact the hosts are usually natives of the place, and the accommodation is their own houses, it can be the optimal way of getting a slice of cultural life. Hotels on the other hand tend to be a duller version of this experience as many are fundamentally the same across various chains and locations.

Cost-effective

The stay can be relatively cheaper than a desired quality hotel. The primary reason being hotels tend to have certain hidden fees that boost up the cost of stay.

Personalized

The accommodation is much more styled to guests preferences. You see, we go on trips for momentary periods in a year, making these moments valuable. In this time, we prefer to put precedence on our wants and desires, more than our needs. The Airbnb staycations allows the user to select from a myriad of options like standout architectural-design homes or lakeside trailers in the middle of nature. Hotels and Inns are largely limited to their area and provide services that are generalized across the board.

Safety, verification, and feedback

The clean style of the platform provides a segment of guest feedback about their stay. The opportunity of a positive-feedback loop is linked with the potential for continuous earnings and future rentals. In the process, building an expectation from the hosts to attempt to provide stellar service and a wholesome experience for each and every stay as one bad review could raise a sense of doubt in the minds of future guests.

The safety feature is backed up by Airbnbs strict procedure of verifying identities for both its hosts and guests. The requirement of uploading a valid ID from both stakeholders creates a requirement of best practice from both ends as any discrepancies can be penalized to the full extent of the law.

The payment procedures are conducted through a safe and secured mechanism which the company takes full responsibility for. It ensures the money is changing hands in an efficient manner, while accounting for their fee.

The space for group travel

If not one of the main attractions, it stands as the one of the top reasons for guests choosing Airbnbs. The fact remains that traveling with a congregation of people and managing separate reservations can be a real headache. Just imagine, the last family trip a decade ago involved separate rooms and bookings, additional costs such as the use of extra beds, and so on. The platform by Airbnb allows you to choose the number of guests and offers accommodations which it can host accordingly. Yes, at a higher rate than your two-person stay, but all under one roof!

Similarly, the stress and frustration of figuring out the three meals of the day can be a massive hassle for most large groups. A significant portion of these large groups' homes have an operating kitchen that enables guests to save on the expenditure of planning meals from outside.

Research Findings

To put numbers to this buzz-worthy name, researchers have attempted to identify reasons behind the demand for Airbnbs. Moreso, the effects of Airbnb's growth in the hospitality industry, and their disrupting effects on long-playing hotel giants who have been the reigning stakeholders.

A survey conducted by Daniel Guttentag, Assistant Professor in Hospitality and Tourism Management at Ryerson University (2016), aimed to study the motivations behind travelers planning stays from the online giant. The method was a 10-minute online survey of 844 respondents who had stayed at an Airbnb in the last 12 months.

According to the research, 80% of the respondents' reasons for booking Airbnb was leisure, and most of them were a group of two to three, and the motivation behind booking via the platform was its low-cost effectiveness. The study went on to state that the practical qualities of the Airbnbs, such as cost, amenities, and convenience, better suited their requirements. Whereas the virtues of host interaction, shared spaces, and culture were important but not the significant reason.

An interesting anecdote that Airbnb boasts about is how the company caters to the more backpacking style of travelers. However, the research found the common guests to be in the category of couples, singles, or small groups. These categories of travelers, therefore, do not necessarily fall under the paradigm of backpacking and more towards seeking a getaway (Guttentag, 2016). According to EHL Insights (n.d.), the findings contradict the marketing ideologies that the company promotes, and debunks the image and perceptions held by the rest of the hospitality and tourism industry regarding customers opting for Airbnb as their arrangement.

An interesting insight into the hospitality industry has provided some key findings. For starters, demand for hotels and other accommodations are expected t0 finally reach the pre-pandemic levels of demand. Here are the figures below as per EHL Insights (2022) statistics:

- hotel occupancy to grow at a rate of 63.4%
- global hospitality growth is expected to reach a compound annual-growth rate (CAGR) of 15.1% after lifting Covid-19 restrictions
- majority of business received is from leisure—business and leisure trips
- Airbnb's revenue to increase by 76.6% from 2020

Pre-pandemic there was a sense of hostility that was seen in this industry towards Airbnb. The hostility and averseness came from reigning hotel giants, such as Marriott and Hilton, who expressed concerns over the disruptions brought on by the tech giant. They stated that the company is over-stretching the rental-market space and making it open for more travelers in the lower-income strata. While this is a good sign for economic growth and the overall tourist industry, certain associations, like American Hotel and Lodging Associations (AHLA), in the hospitality industry seem to consider it a threat—irrespective of the fact that they serve different cohorts of the populace. Conversely, we have boutique designer hotels who have partnered up with Airbnb to list their rooms. This is a positive sign of adaptation and versatility.

Being The Host

The current trend in many social-media platforms showcase individuals who have freed themselves from the restraints of day-to-day work-life through the Airbnb platform. They share their success stories of enlisting their properties or managing enlisted properties on the platform. The earnings from the properties have generated enough cash flow to cover the needs and free up their time to live a desirable life of their own choice. While this perceptibility of generating substantial income from Airbnb rentals is true and possible, one must consider their individual circumstances before considering opting for this venture. In a nutshell, there are three variants of hosts that have emerged in the trade: opportunist, steady-income seeker, and full-time entrepreneur. Opportunists seek to put up their rentals based on certain time intervals. They look out for prospective festivals, events, religious holidays, or peak seasons to cash in on high demand. The fact remains that, like small intervals of rental stays, they too are in it for the short term—more specifically, time intervals. The steady-income host plans to entertain guests over consistent weekends or dedicated intervals of the month. They aim to maximize on moments of high demands and prefer consistency of short-term stays over long-term renters. Finally, we have the full-time host who wishes to dedicate the earnings from their Airbnb units as their primary income source. Famously known as rentrepreneurs, these individuals have enlisted certain units just for rentals—whether it be for short or long-time intervals. These classifications are a barometer in gauging one's own individual needs and possible aims when considering hosting.

The hard work behind this lifestyle is often not clarified in the buzzing posts of these self-made people. One's own prevailing state of income, savings, daily expenses, familial responsibilities, and lifestyle habits will influence the outcome of profiting from Airbnb rentals. At the end of the day, success is a multifaceted outcome, and an over-ambitious drive without careful planning can prove to be catastrophic. The Airbnb website consists of multiple short-read resources for potential parties considering hosting. The scripts encourage the art of hosting, citing success stories and insights into best practices. So, what should you be considering before diving into the world of hosting?

Duties and Responsibilities

Do you have the space?

Essentials in listings require the hosts to provide a sleeping space, whether that be a room or area with an access to a bathroom. Both the areas must be clean and usable for the guests at the very least. The factor of space is imperative for this hustle to work out. If an individual has a property separate from their own home, that's great! Similarly, if they have a separate section with a private access that they can rent out, that also works! On the other hand, if you do not have the abovementioned luxuries, that's completely alright and can still consider listing—at the expense of privacy that is. See, you have to consider sharing your personal space with strangers; verified, yes, but strangers, nonetheless.

It can be a full-time job

The practice can take up a whole lot of your daily schedule and can prove to be draining initially. Taking on hosting on your own would mean managing booking requests, responding to queries on the app, re-stocking amenities, cleaning the apartments after every stay, and so on. The aspect of cleaning can become a hassle and time consuming on your own, especially if hiring outside services eat up on your profits too much. Finally, if you are holding a full-time job, the overall practice can become brutal and might require hiring assistants at the very least to help.

Behavioral practices and house etiquette

Adding to the point of sharing space, an individual also needs to take on a newfound behavior mindset when it comes to hosting people. These guests are paying for this stay and are expectant of decent service from the host. That equates to maintaining decorum in the house, ensuring noise levels are at a permissible level, other family members are compliant of the guests and so on. If they have access to the kitchen and the fridge, ensuring there is enough space available to store their food and be able to cook as they desire. These aspects, though small, can be the defining feature of the success a shared-space host might have.

Accounting for damage and disruptions

Okay so, not everyone is a saint, and while one hopes to have their fair share of dream guests, they will encounter the potential outliers. Yes, Airbnb does have a plan for this, called AirCoverage, which is free and applied towards hosts. However, they apply if the host is the prime owner of the property, and therefore, not in cases of Airbnb arbitrage practices (which we will cover in other chapters). As per TurnoverBnB (2022), AirCoverage umbrella covers physical damage or loss caused by the guests during the stay (including damage from pets), unforeseen cleaning expenses, and income loss from canceled reservations due to damage. However, they're limited to further loopholes such as damage caused after the duration of stay has ended, loss of valuables by the guests, natural calamities, and so on. Just like every insurance policy, they're susceptible to loopholes that can harm the hosts—hence, being aware of the protection umbrella is crucial. Finally, policies in your neighborhood can require hosts to take up additional insurance policies such as homeowners or business insurance; more of this will be covered in the subsequent chapters.

Snarky reviews are evident

No matter how great you are as a host, it might be that your splendor, service, and behavior has fallen short in the eyes of your guests. The only opportunity here is to learn from the feedback, and possibly, adapt to it. Especially when it comes to aspects of the property, or in the host's approach with guests.

Being compliant with your neighbors and community

House rules for the listing should be drawn out while considering the surrounding community and neighbors. Loud music, disruptions, littering, and violence can prove to be a nuisance, and put a black mark on your property. Worst case scenario, it can lead to dealing with law enforcement if the issues are too severe.

Rewards

The above-mentioned points can very well be considered a comprehensive list of duties Airbnb hosts are expected to undertake. These tasks can prove to be time-consuming and difficult with limited potential for positive developments in the short term. On the bright side, anything worthwhile comes with responsibilities, and at the end of the daily hustle of hosting, lies the sunny side with potential and success.

Income generation

The hustle into venturing towards hosting can generate substantial financial gains for the host. Quite likely, this factor stays as the significant motivator for considering this trade. The scope for income can be assessed with the help of platforms such as the AirDNA market finder. The system allows you to gauge the income stream generated in the area you are residing with statistical insights into average per-night income, booking rates, incoming traffic, and so on. Additionally, you can even search the exact address of your property and figure out the effective rate that can be charged in respect to your location, and apartment size. Starting out on the Airbnb platform, hosts do not need to pay any fees to list their property. This can be a real attraction as the entry costs are basically nil.

Verified guests through the platform

The fact that Airbnb verifies and requires guests to provide photo ID soothes the trust issues from harboring strangers under your roof. Also, uploading valid identification pegs them to ensure the best behavior during their stay as any diversion from the status quo can possibly lead to strenuous actions on the guests.

Platform efficacy

The Airbnb application offers a seamless means of promoting your property to millions of avid guests worldwide, handle booking, seek queries from customer support, and receive due payments—all with the platform. The overall features come at a marginal cost to the host as Airbnb only takes a certain percentage as their service fee.

Potential for growth

The newest features in the Airbnb platform customizes the listings with neighboring area activities. This really aids in the advertisement features of the listing and makes it more desirable. Therefore, the rental market for short-term staycations is seen to project an upward growth. Jumping in on this trend holds the opportunity for exponential growth and subsequent income generation. Expenditure on your rentals is usually seen to be directly correlated with higher cash flow—a motivator for creating an ambience of prime living for the hosts. While many see this is a deterrent, any business requires reinvesting profits back into it to scale the growth further.

Hosts set their own prices

A striking difference from other peer-to-peer platforms, Airbnb allows its hosts to set their own prices. While setting realistic prices are expected, hosts appreciate this convenience as they can value and adjust prices in accordance with the bookings. Additionally, in the case of long-term rentals, hosts have the opportunity to offer lucrative discounts to make them stand out more.

The insurance and rights

Just as this was a barrier, on the flipside, it's also a great lifesaver for hosts as it fundamentally offers a sense of protection for homeowners. Houses are precious, and the fact that Airbnb offers this feature at no additional cost to its hosts really shows that the company cares for its stakeholders.

So, Why Host?

The real question should be, why not host? As we have learned, the preferences for booking Airbnbs are numerous. The platform's quality, as an ever-changing landscape that is open to new styles of hosting, attracts its own unique types of guests. We mentioned the practice of guests who give favor to their desires more than their needs during vacations or trips as these make up small moments compared to the rest of the year. Similarly, considering yourself as a new host, and developing your own uniqueness in your rentals can create a sense of attraction to many guests operating in the platform—finding the right people as per your services.

We also learned that figures can be misleading, and people often seek the convenience of low cost and accessibility over other aspects when it comes to their housing. Considering your locality as a place of a high traffic area of activities, a combination of decent service in a busy place can even work.

Finally, we spoke about the pros and cons of hosting. As mentioned before, anything worthwhile always comes at a cost. Starting your own Airbnb journey can be daunting at first, however, gauging the inherent possibilities of financial gain is always present and a real attraction.

CHAPTER 2
RULES IN PLACE

The market for short-term rentals has boomed since the emergence of Airbnb in 2016. More and more people have considered hosting, and as the popularity grew, more and more guests have considered using it as a means for accommodation. Like everything else, growth always accompanies spillovers—both positive and negative in nature.

Considering the possibility of unexpected emergencies, the company has administered a set of rules and best practices. On the other hand, the city or state you are operating in can hold their own laws and policies that can influence the outcome of your listings.

There's a section under the Airbnb website that points towards responsible hosting in the United States. The information in this segment outlines a hearty list of practices that serve to tackle unexpected outcomes. For instance, the top five categories include health and cleanliness, safety, permissions, neighbors, and local regulations (n.d.).

Health and cleanliness

The section covers the set of guidelines for cleaning the rentals after each booking as declared by the Center of Disease Control (CDC). It, additionally, involves the requirement for barring the entry of new guests before the disinfection process is complete. Also, after the prevalence of Covid-19, more stringent measures have been adopted since declared by the US Environmental Protection Agency (EPA). Cleaning guidelines and practices will be further covered in the subsequent chapters.

Safety

The aspect of safety, as mentioned in the previous chapters, is imperative, both for the guests and the hosts. Under safety procedures, routine practices would be to install smoke detectors and fire alarms. Smoke detectors can aid in tracking smoking issues too, which can also oftentimes be a rule set by a host. Additionally, many of the guests can be from out of town and even completely different countries. Providing a document of emergency contact information in the area can be largely beneficial at times of crisis. Furthermore, in the case of fires, having valid fire extinguishers and mapped out exit paths (if available) can be a life saver—nowadays most buildings are required by law to house the basic fire prevention means.

Hazards

We're all at the mercy of Mother Nature and its adverse outcomes during times of natural disaster. Hence, having a home that can withstand the whims of nature is essential. Similarly, if listings are usually made throughout the year, and the location of operation is prone to bouts of cold, having a stable heating system and hot water line is crucial.

Conversely, scoping your home for potential accidents should also be conducted. A loose nail on a floorboard, broken steps, live wires, and so on can be a serious health risk or open to cases of injury. Regardless of the rules in place by Airbnb that covers injuries of guests during the stay, no one would want such a scenario arising. Also, if you feel the house might see bookings from families, childproofing certain hazardous parts of the home can be great.

Neighbors

Having a rental in a building can mean accounting for your neighbors. Generally, all guests have luggage, and might be unaware of the noise while dragging it through the stairs and across hallways. On the other hand, we have the common noise complaints from parties, loud music, and so on. Simply put, Airbnb hosts need to clarify house rules very clearly before any bookings are placed and money exchanges hands. Thus, in times of issues, hosts and guests can refer very easily to said rules.

Permissions and local regulations

Finally, we have the aspect of laws and regulations. If you're a host who's wishing to sublet your own rented property, you should definitely go through the lease terms before making any decisions because there's a chance you might be breaking a law. You see, many Homeowners Associations (HOA) or co-op boards bar renters from sub-letting their apartments for short-term stays. The reasons for this could be numerous: damage, nuisance, safety concerns, and so on—all very valid reasons. In the case of local laws, many areas and towns can limit or act as a deterrent to Airbnb rentals due to similar reasons of safety and damages. For the US, Airbnb website holds a comprehensive list of local-law regulations as per the towns where they operate. A new host should research the laws concerning their locality before jumping into this venture.

Here is an overview of laws and regulations of some of the prominent states and their cities regarding Airbnb and other short-term rentals.

For the case of Los Angeles, Airbnb regulations involve registering a property with the city, and paying a home-sharing fee. This allows the host to be able to entertain guests for up to 120 nights annually. In addition, they add a 14% tax called the transient occupancy tax (i.e., short-term stay tax.) This is on top of the cleaning and service fee, and therefore, adds to the overall cost of the guests. Finally, if any host wishes to entertain longer than 120 nights annually, they must register for an extended home-sharing permit from the city at a higher cost. Similar cases are there for other cities like San Francisco and Santa Monica, California.

In the case of New York City, the restrictions for Airbnb are quite stringent. There's the multiple dwelling law (MDL) which limits hosting restrictions for apartment units. Basically, MDL does not allow stays for durations of less than a month for housing which has three or more apartment units—known as Class A dwellings. There is an inherent risk of privacy or sharing personal data as Airbnb is required to share listing data along with in-app guest details to the city for listings shorter than 30 days. After all that, listings from a one house unit may have to meet extensive zoning restrictions, and health and safety codes. Without which, permission may not be granted for hosting and fines may be levied if continued to do so.

In the case of Las Vegas, the rules are pretty unusual. For starters, hosts have to be owners of the property, and thus, eliminates the opportunities for subletting and Airbnb arbitrage. On top of that, the insurance policies require hosts to have business licenses, and add $500,000 liability insurance. Interestingly, they have to collect taxes from the guests and send it back to the city. Lastly, their unit location requirements do not allow two rental properties to be registered close to each other! The city has a limit that does not allow more than two adults to stay in one room. Alongside that is the further restrictions as to the number of rooms a single rental unit can have to qualify as a viable Airbnb listing.

Know Your Customers, Know Your Market

Knowing your market is as important as knowing your customer and vice versa. The point of this is gaining knowledge and insights into both categories that will give you an entrepreneurial edge over others. The insights from these categories can overlap into each other as they both eventually affect the outcome of the other—decent markets and areas attract decent guests, and an influx of decent guests into an area builds a newfound attractive market.

In the world of real-estate investment, a go-to research practice involves conducting a renter's market analysis. This would involve looking into various factors such as market capitalization, identifying positive factors of the neighborhood, determining price as per the locality, and so on. However, the case of Airbnb rental analysis is different from the general real-estate investment. As compared to a normal rental analysis, Airbnb stays are much more short-term and are not lease intensive—guests usually sign a lease of monthly, half-yearly, or annual lease in general-market rentals.

Manual Analysis

A manual analysis of the Airbnb market analysis is broken down into multiple steps. Let us go into the process and identify key points to consider as stated by Zaragoza (2021):

Figuring out the city

This step is fundamental, as your city will largely influence your success when you venture into this field. A city which enriches the aspect of the Airbnb experience is sought after, and if your city falls short on certain criteria, it's alright to move forward to consider others.

Considering your city or locality is a healthy environment for such a venture, we can consider the first aspect of seasons. In starting your venture, you might notice the demand for your listings and the overall accommodation rates of the short-term rentals in your area might be cyclical in nature. In other words, the demand might be more seasonal. This means, certain times of the year might see an influx of tourists, travelers, vacationers, and locals coming into the city for short-term stays. Other times, it might be relatively slow. If your area is more sporting for the summer vibes, you will see a high influx of tourists and subsequent bookings starting from spring through fall. While this may mean business is not consistent, it could hold the opportunity for cashing double during the peak seasons—so much so that it covers the dormant months of the year.

Your area could house significant local events that can attract people from all over the world. Consider the La Tomatina festival held in the small town of Valencian in Bunol, Spain. The northern light festival of Norway and Iceland and even the full moon party on the island of Koh Pha-Ngan in Thailand. All these events attract hordes of guests from all over the world who all require a place to stay. Most of these city events are available in the event calendar of your local government websites and worth keeping track of. Similarly, certain websites and companies create updates that you can sign up to for upcoming events near your area.

Being comfortable with the rules and regulations

Something which cannot be emphasized further is being aware of the local laws. These can make or break your career before it even takes off. Fines can be expensive and can put a black mark on your listing if it represents as an inconvenience for your guests.

Accessibility and safety

Apart from the actual stay, your guests are equally enamored by the locality. It has even been seen via research that guests hardly stay at the room apart from using it at night for sleep. A key characteristic is a walkability score which gives an index of high (walker's paradise) and low (long and strenuous walks) to an area, in terms of the duration to access key areas of the locality. A high walkability score can be advertised on your listing which, believe it or not, can be quite the trump card. Similarly, accessibility to the downtown area, shops, malls, boardwalks, beaches, parks, and business centers are attractive depending on the type of guests you're hosting.

Finally, the issue of safety as always is key to success in hosting. A single incident of burglary or mugging can taint the reputation of your listing in the form of a bad review. Thus, being aware of your area's crime index can allow you to make more clear decisions.

Social-media hosting groups

There's bound to be at least one group on a social-media platform, like Facebook, Instagram, or Twitter, where a hosting group is present. Joining one of these groups can help you gauge your markets better. Many of these groups have trimester meet-ups where they discuss issues, network, and help each other out. Yes, they're also your competition, but at the end of the day, all of you are on the same boat.

Guest analysis

This type of guest analysis involves the stream of individuals and their background who take on bookings in your area. This is linked to the aspect of your neighborhood's characteristics as the guests are usually the ones who are drawn to those characteristics.

Price benchmarking

This is best done through a competitor's analysis. For instance, evaluating similar homes and their prices to determine your own strategies. The best practice as stated by Zaragoza (2021) "You would want to find at least three direct competitors. If you're struggling to find this many competitors, try finding out why. It may turn out that there is zero demand for that type of property in that area."

Investment Analysis Tool

AirDNA

Coming to online tools, one of the prominent software solutions available to potential hosts is the AirDNA. The tool can be used to assess the markets you wish to operate in by analyzing the competitors present. Therefore, it can give you an extensive forecast of revenue generation if you consider venturing into the market. The tool comes in both free and premium versions for its members. The premium tool lets its users access quantitative analytics into the market, competitors, and guests. The subscription packages range from $10–50 per month depending on your market (Griffiths, 2021). In terms of price setting, a comprehensive feature of AirDNA is the rentalizer tool. The feature, which also serves as an Airbnb financial calculator, gives its user the insight into potential revenue generation on specific addresses. The revenue model can give you an annual forecast along with expected booking rates.

Let us give you a brief overview of the tool and what to expect from it. The data analytics tool, which was started in 2015, came with two prominent features of understanding the market with its analysis of competitors (Market Minder), and the opportunity to forecast potential investment growth (Investment Explorer). However, they recently removed the investment explorer tool and launched three new tiers with increased pricing segments. The landing page, after you access your account, will give you the main market metrics of occupancy, revenue, demand of the area, and so on. Another feature called the market grade gives out a score between 0–100 to a market based on parameters established by them. The factors include regulations, demand growth, rental occupancy rates, and so on. A score between 80–85 for a city is considered an attractive area and can be expectant of higher demand and guest traffic. Active daily rates and occupancy rates give insights on the average price of rentals and average booking rate, respectively. Other sections include active rentals, rentalizer, seasonality predictions, and lead time. Active rentals give you a snapshot of the type of rental properties booked in your area, whether it be a one room, condo, full house, and so on. As mentioned before, rentalizer helps you project your financials and the return on investments (ROIs). Seasonality predicts peak-demand seasons over an annual period. Finally, lead time allows you to be aware of booking to check the wait time of your guests and helps in the time management of maintaining and re-preparing the rentals for future guests.

The system is not flawless, and with all software, it comes with drawbacks. The AirDNA analytics is not based on real-time data. They usually collect data through scouring the Airbnb website for rentals, bookings, guest types, and so on. As per

Kaushik (2021), the website only updates its data 12 times a year or once every month. This can be frightfully problematic for high-volume hosts who assess their listings based on the previous month's data. The review of the website is mostly on the grounds of cost effectiveness. Yes, cost of the service does play a part, however, it's minuscule to the monthly-revenue generation from hosting multiple units. Therefore, scouring the Airbnb website reviews of hosts, you will evidently find mixed reviews of the tool. Finally, not all of the areas and localities are present on the platform. All these issues make any attempt to make a short-term decision using the platform very troublesome.

Mashvisor

Mashvisor is another well-liked real-estate analyzer tool. Based on performance characteristics and any current promotional offers in the area, the property tool enables its investors to purchase prominent real estate in a certain location. The performance reflects two facets, both short-term and long-term leasing.

Mashvisor obtains data through a variety of channels and refines the data from multiple sources to ensure its authenticity. Realtor.com, Zillow, MLS, Airbnb, Auciton.com, Roofstock, and others are some of their sources (Kaushik, 2021). Websites such as Realtor.com, Zillow, and MLS make property information publicly available. Physical description, previous owner history, price, and size are all included. Mashvisor predicts short-term rental income of properties using data from the short-term rental market provided by Airbnb. Similarly, Roofstock assists in the acquisition of single-family homes with a guaranteed minimum rent.

Mashvisor's user interface and data have significantly improved over the past seven years. The dashboard is incredibly user-friendly. It shouldn't be challenging for a novice to rapidly become accustomed to the dashboard. The search function's color-coded "heatmap" is particularly helpful. The results are displayed in two shades—red and green; where red indicates low and green indicates high users. The system is then able to sort per the metrics of listing price, cap rate, or cash returns (Kaushik, 2021). The search metrics can be changed at will by a user using specific search criteria.

To make sure the properties found using the Property Finder satisfy a specific investor's need for minimum returns, more analysis should be conducted on them. Usually, the procedure involves creating a spreadsheet with potential revenues, costs, and cash flows. For people who don't frequently work with spreadsheets, producing something similar can prove challenging. The system of property analysis is built upon a model that enables investors to determine the key factors of income, return on investments, and market capitalizations. Investors frequently overestimate income and underestimate expenses, which results in errors in the estimates. Through the system of generating revenue figures from information obtained through the Property Search feature and estimating expenditures (both initial and continuing) based on averages for comparable properties in the database, the model reduces the possibility of significant inaccuracies. With the help of the program, users can modify each component to produce a customized worksheet that better predicts future outcomes. Investors can identify the optimal use of a potential property with the aid of Mashvisor's analysis modeling. It contrasts the financial results of long-term leasing against short-term Airbnb rentals. Short-term rentals aren't always the best investments in certain areas! To make the best decision, I believe that the Property Analysis model successfully transforms a typically complicated project into an elegant, transparent, and auditable result.

Airbtics

Airbtics is another software that has become quite popular amongst hosts. The software integrates data using historical points in time, and gives you a better presentation regarding investment, pricing, and listing strategies. The software is built to identify market gaps and be able to point them out.

The issue with Airbtics is that they require a one-time payment which can be relatively high. Initially, it might be a deterrent to new users, but over time this can prove to be a cheaper and better alternative throughout.

Pricing Strategies

The price, relative to all the other factors, can be considered as the first thing the average guest will notice. They're usually the first factor that aids the guest in making an unconscious decision of considering the property. Almost all of us travel at a set budget and leave room for deviating from it here and there. Accommodation for most guests is the highest expenditure segment, and if the prices do not reflect the value they will be getting, you can be quite sure your booking rate will be sparse. Therefore, a pricing strategy that reflects the strengths of your listing is imperative. Below are points to consider while setting up your pricing strategies:

Location

Locations are the first step in setting up the pricing strategy. At the end of the day, your listing is a physical property located in a particular area. Each area has their unique traits and attributes that ascend its value in comparison to others. Similarly, these attributes aid in inflating the prices you can charge. As we have mentioned in the previous segment, doing a renters' analysis will help you gauge the prevailing rates in the market you wish to be based in. A proper host will consider its competitors' rates and use that to set their rate—not as a direct linkage to the price as there are other factors to consider too.

Listing type

The number of bedrooms, washrooms, kitchen access, floor space, backyard access, washer/dryer in-unit—all these factors add to the price listed. A competitor might have a two-bedroom apartment but does not provide kitchen and washer/dryer access. Therefore, allowing this service would equate to marginally higher prices than theirs. Similarly, it's a common practice for hosts to charge rates slightly lower than its competitors for similar listings to attract more guests and have the venture take off.

Covering the cost

While you may be considering lower rates than the market, it could drag you out of business. Yes, it's important to stay competitive, but not at the cost of only breaking even or losing money. A significant part of success in the Airbnb business involves re-investing profits back into it—as a means of increasing the value of your service. Therefore, pricing strategies should, at the very least, account for your fixed and variable expenses with some margin for cash in pocket, and if possible, investment.

Market segments

Using adaptive tools like Mashvisor, AirDNA, or Airbtics will also give you insights into your guest types. This opens room to strategize your pricing blueprint based on this info. If the listings are providing high-end value and opulent living, the rate should very much match that. While, on the other hand, listings that are more directed towards low-cost alternatives for students, businesspeople, etc., the pricing should be indicative of it.

The Airbnb platform

As stated earlier, hosts are given complete authority in setting their own rates. The Airbnb platform has certain built-in tools that aid in this process. It starts out by providing a basal rate to your listing that may not be an accurate measure or strategy. As stated by Riddles (2021), "The Airbnb Smart Pricing tool is another option designed to automate your pricing based on demand and supply, property type and amenities, local events, reviews, and other data relevant to your listing."

Regulations and taxes

This is a common topic of discussion whenever we dive deep into Airbnb hosting. The pricing strategies should account for your area's regulations, laws, rules, and city taxes. Taxes could ultimately eat your profit, and as we've seen, some cities and states charge exorbitant rates. Finally, local regulation, if not directly then indirectly, affects your profits by influencing occupancy rates. Therefore, hosts should very much consider the regulations in place when considering pricing strategy.

Variable components

The Airbnb platform has certain components which inadvertently contribute to the hosts' profit levels. The fact that these components are variable makes it important for hosts to have a steady track of them.

Cleaning fees are inclusive in the final price a guest will pay but will not be stated in the original listing price on the platform. For instance, a listing might go for $50 per night, but accounting for the cleaning fee and taxes, end up at $100 per night. Now, cleaning fees vary and have recently been hiked by the company (covered more in a later chapter). The fact remains that the host should be aware of this change, and if needed, slightly adjust prices in the short run to take advantage of the elastic demand.

Extra charges are aspects that push up average rates of a listing. They usually come as everyday housekeeping services, hiring cooks, using the host's properties such as boats and so on. Or could be presented as allowing an extra guest to be added. While both these factors add up for the pockets of the guest, a host must decide whether they would allow these luxuries in the first place. An extra guest means faster depletion of supplies and amenities. Hiring external service providers involves the hassle of booking them and figuring out the logistics.

Security deposits are sometimes charged by hosts as a means to cover any unforeseen damage caused by guests. These are usually the case when the guests are interested in making use of a particular asset like a boat or car. These deposits are refundable and paid out after a successful and damage-free stay.

Discounts are another aspect that the host can avail to set their final prices. Usually, the practice involves offering discounts for any stay of seven days or more. Taking advantage of the discount rates can aid in attracting more guests.

All these factors will help a host in gauging their nightly rate. All in all, hosts even have the opportunity to break up the listing as single rooms in the same apartment or the entire unit as whole for maximum number of tenants.

Starting an LLC

We have learned the means through which hosts can possibly secure their properties, valuables, rent, and unforeseen circumstances. However, there lies a final approach that can really put the "nail in the coffin" (i.e., secure your property and earnings.)

A prerequisite to holding success for hosts is to establish a limited liability company (LLC) for their rental business. However, what's an LLC and why's it relevant here? Starting out, an LLC is considered a hybrid entity in the business realm. As like a corporation, it protects its owners from liability if the company fails, and as a partnership entity, through its pass-through profit structure where taxes are charged after they have disbursed to its owners (Fernando, 2022). The entity is rather open to the type of owners it can have from foreigners, foreign companies, individuals, and corporations, with the exception of banking and insurance services. It's true that the rules for starting an LLC vary between states. Finally, it's a formal business entity that has to submit formal legal documents with its home state and defines clear roles of the owners/members, duties, liabilities, and goals.

Pros and Cons

Now that we have a broad definition on the scope and objectives of an LLC, let us apply the same into our topic of Airbnb hosting. Like the above advantages of the entity, Airbnb hosts can capitalize on the benefits of liability protection, tax benefits, and more—while at a mere cost of overheads and admin expenses.

Liability protection

Consider an example of a host who has just ventured into the trade of hosting and listed the entirety or a section of their own house on the platform. Or the case of the Airbnb hosts who have scaled up to multiple properties across various geographical locations. Both these cases fall under the protection offered by an LLC. Considering either of the two scenarios and allowing for the variable of an unforeseen accident where a guest is injured—assuming the guest decides to sue, the owner's personal assets of wealth or even the property are not at risk.

The injury claim will have to be filed against the LLC. In the worst-case outcome of the host losing the case (highly unlikely scenario), the entity will be responsible to pay reparations to the injured guest. Of course, Airbnb does have a contingency plan in place that helps protect hosts in the event of guest injuries. However, this is carried out in the expectation that the guests will not consider taking legal action on the host directly as the listing is represented as an LLC.

Tax Benefits

The pass-through system of profit taxation can allow for monumental tax savings on high volumes of cash flows. There are two methods of applying tax on their business earnings with the LLC route, both of which aid in the scope of tax savings. Firstly, taxes are paid after profits are paid out to the owners, and taxes are filed on the personal statement of the owner (Schedule C). This applies for cases of single or multiple-owned LLC entities. Secondly, there is the scope for opening the hosting business as an "S Corporation." This system applies for the case of multiple owners in an LLC and allows for greater savings as profits are taxed after they've been distributed to its shareholders. Therefore, the members can even be hired as employees and have options to earn dividends on shares. In the case of an S corp, possibility for scalability shoots up as re-investment opportunities resurfaces against the tax savings.

Host privacy

A significant aspect of protection that an LLC provides is by adding a layer of security to the owner's personal information. As aforementioned, no host can ever always secure good and positive reviews—there will always be an unsatisfied guest. In the case of any outliers of unsatisfied guests who seek to learn the identity and personal information of the host, such as address, full name, and so on, can very well do so. The means of it can be arranged by going through the public tax records. Hence, forming an LLC would act as the first line of defense as the entity's information would spring up first.

Credibility

Finally, the aspect of credibility is fortified by forming an LLC for an Airbnb business. The primary benefit is that it operates under the business name, instead of the name of its owner. While a host may wish to attach their name to its properties, when it comes to scalability, it can prove to be an unnecessary hassle. You see partnering up with other entities, vendors, or merchants is better possible through representation of the Airbnb trade as an LLC. This is because they tend to take this much more seriously. In the case of seasoned guests and travelers who have had their fair share of unfortunate stays, they also tend to take corporations more seriously than an Airbnb created using the host's name. All in all, credibility is important in ensuring future scalability and trust.

Overall, the benefits of operating an LLC far outweighs the drawbacks. The primary expense endured by individuals lies in the overhead cost and administrative costs during its formation. A large portion of the overhead cost could go into hiring a lawyer to ensure clean and discrepancy-free documents for submitting to the state. The aspect of administrative costs is amplified when it comes to calculating business owners' taxes.

Formation

The means of forming an LLC is fairly straightforward but can seem complicated for first timers. Hence, hiring a professional or seeking expert help eases the burden. The first step would be to have an enlisted name for the trade. The interesting thing here is names are open to take because someone else has not already taken it. Therefore, if you do have a name in mind, making a few Google searches should reveal whether an already-operating LLC is using it. There are certain states that allow for a base fee to hold a name.

The second step involves filing the legal documents, also known as the article of organization, with the state. These documents are usually prepared by attorneys or businesses specializing in LLC formations. These parties gather the documents from the owners and file on their behalf. Apart from the attorney fee, there are usually filing fees that have to be paid.

Next, we have the appointment of a point of contact for the business. This position is critical as they're considered the registered agent for all legal formalities and document handling on behalf of the LLC. The option to be the registered agent is open to the owner, however, not one which is recommended. Attorneys or qualified personnel are usually appointed as registered agents.

Lastly, we have the operations agreement which outlines the rights and responsibilities of the enlisted owners. It fundamentally states the businesses goals, key information, tax treatment practices, process of acquiring new owners, and so on.

There are outlier cases where certain states require the LLC to be published in the newspapers. As stated by Chang (2022) "Three states require business owners to publish a notification of their LLC's formation in newspapers including Arizona, Nebraska and New York." Hosts should still research if there are any additional local rules and regulations pertaining to forming LLCs. Also, if there are any limitations present with LLCs for housing and short-term rentals.

Host Essentials

In this comprehensive chapter, we have described the importance of knowing your customers and knowing your markets. We have discussed relevant means of learning the market and its attributes—manually and through automated investment tools. We further detailed three key investment tools and their own relevance in the current markets.

The core practice of pricing strategies was covered in this segment. The depth of the pricing strategies is dependent on many factors that a potential host needs to consider.

Lastly, we delved into the significance of forming an LLC for an Airbnb business. We specified the means through which an LLC can protect its host's privacy and liability risk, allow for tax benefits, and give more credibility. Also, we included a section on how to form an LLC.

CHAPTER 3

SETTING UP FOR SUCCESS

S ince the emergence of Airbnb rentals, it's in direct competition with the hospitality business. From motels to inns, 7-star luxury hotels, and your bed and breakfasts—Airbnb offers unique experiences as per the aforementioned segments and many, many more. This does not take away from the fact that the businesses here have been around for much longer and have quite perfected their art of guest-stay experiences. They incorporate certain practices and virtues that have been around for a long time now. Essentially, these practices have cemented themselves in the minds of our guests, and through which they gauge the worthiness of new places of accommodations. Airbnb rentals are, thus, very much in the target of judgment as per these criteria. So, what are these essential practices?

The Proper in Property

Securing a ready property in a great location is definitely the starting point. However, garnering solid reviews and positive feedback from guests are the game of optimal experiences in hospitality. It's the name of the industry and niche that separates a host from every other player in the industry. Being an Airbnb host means more than just providing a place to crash for your guests. The platform boasts about its surreal experience of accommodation, and the hosts are on the heels of this art. Here are the means of ensuring efficacy of your accommodation as per the best practices of the industry.

Safety and childproofing

Let us consider the first of the requirements for all human beings, safety. A safe haven is usually your own home. During vacations, they're your accommodations. Airbnbs listed have to be safe or create the perception of safety. The structures must be built to withstand the variations of mother nature. It must accommodate for shelter for the extremities of weather. It must be able to provide safety from nature's wilderness and its inhabitants. Interior wise, any broken floorboard, leaky faucets, live wires, or broken pipes need to be amended. Lastly, childproofing, if not an essential, is a recommended practice. Yes, your usual guests could be adults. However, first-time families are not uncommon, and the extra mile can be extremely favorable, and open a new niche for your listing.

Cleanliness

You know the cliché "cleanliness is next to godliness"? It might not be necessarily true for a higher ascension in the afterlife, but it's definitely relevant in securing a habitat of excellent accommodation reviews. Hygiene is a sought-after practice and a deal breaker in the industry. Guests are aware that their place of stay has been inhabited beforehand, no one is denying this truth. The art is mimicking the illusion for each and every stay. It's as if the accommodation has been reinvested or catered just for the new guests. As stated by Get Paid For Your Pad (2019) "You are competing with hotels and luxury brands, even the worst hotels have this basic standard of service. You have to be sure this is done every time." In the later segment of this chapter, we will delve into the list of amenities that are essential for hygiene practice in an Airbnb listing.

Decor

This shows creativity and personalization of the host and creates a sense of belonging. Decor adds life to your home and gives the guest a taste of your background, culture, and lifestyle. Thus, transforming the decor and building towards it is the best practice. Also, decorating as per the current themes (seasons, holidays) adds further touches which makes the listing standout.

Best practices

Before making the listing available, it's a very good idea to remove all personal belongings that will not be useful to the guest. This is especially true if you are listing your own home. Personal items could include jewelry, valuable arts, legal and personal documents, and so on.

On the other hand, providing a handful of your own items for temporary use could work great! Starting with a local directory, magazines, board games, easy local translations, appliance-use manuals, and so on.

Amending Your Amenities

Amenities are useful features that aid in the quality of service offered by an accommodation. Here we categorize the amenities by sections of the accommodation to better clarify it. The categories do not encompass all the sections of the house and are open for further additions or removals.

Bedroom

This is the room which has been primarily used by guests. The bedroom is a personal space and should hold aspects of comfort, aesthetics, and sleep in its ambiance. Starting with the bed itself, pillows with allergy-free covers are relevant. There should be at least one pillow per guest in the room. Clean bed sheets with duvet covers and blankets are essential. Also, a side table with a bedside lamp and drawers for personal storage are important features. Adding to the touch, an alarm clock, extension cords for charging devices, and additional outlets around the bed really add to the convenience. Hosting for families, a small baby crib can really add a sense of value to the guests. On top of that, access to extra pillows and air mattresses will be greatly appreciated. In the closet, access to extra hangers, iron, and ironing boards are great and cost-effective add-ons.

Overall, adding to the decor can really pay off for hosts. This is because it creates a perception of luxury and value to the guests which can be a means of charging more for your listing. Simple aspects of adding wall art, high-quality linen sheets, and statement pieces boost the perceptive value.

Bathroom

As stated by Ward (2019), "A bathroom should be a place of sanctuary and relaxation and making this happen is a surefire way of earning extra brownie points." Essentially the bathroom should be spotless and have a range of access to basic hygiene amenities. The shower experience can be a great way for generating an essence of high service to the guests. Optimal shower experience can be created with a high-quality shower head with multiple water-output options. Access to a shower gel, shampoo, conditioner, and body oils are a must. An essential requirement is having access to hot water, and a proper shower curtain or door that separates the area from the rest of the washroom. Multiple towels including face, hand, and body towels are great add ons. A slip-resistant mat inside the shower area is a great safety tool. A drying carpet outside the shower area adds to the value. Finally, toilet paper, bidets, and aroma diffusers are practical and necessary. To enhance the experience, you can add a set of fresh toothbrushes, and one-time razor kits at cheap prices—as these are usual items the guests forget to pack. Hair dryers and curlers are beneficial to guests as these can be bulky items to carry. Finally, a personal favorite is adding two bathrobes which really add to the sense of luxury.

Kitchen

A big reason for opting for Airbnb over other accommodations lies in the access to the kitchen. Food is a major component of expenditure for guests. Apart from your traditional complimentary breakfasts at certain hotels, guests usually arrange meals from outside sources. Yes, it's part of the vacationing experience, but it can leave a toll on the wallet. Therefore, a cost-effective option would be cooking at home for certain meals. Additionally, many families prefer this over outside food.

Starting off, your kitchen needs to be equipped with the basic set of appliances. A working stove (electrical or gas), oven, microwave, air fryer, fridge, sink, etc. are essential. Having access to a dishwasher can be quite convenient too. In terms of cooking utensils, providing sets of pots and pans with ladles and whisks are important. A set of kitchen towels, oven mitts, and aprons are great add-ons. Finally, cooking oils and stocking up on essentials such as sugar, salt, and certain key spices are a best practice. If you're worried about overconsumption, you can create a way to keep track of the amount available before and after the stay. Usually, guests use minimal amounts of the stocks, and have been seen to cook, on average, one meal a day. Adding to the luxury stay, having a coffee maker really works. A personal preference would be providing an option of water filter or a Britta-filter jug as many guests might not opt for tap water.

Lounge and Living Rooms

Starting off, an access to a lounge area gives a high sense of value to the guest. It's because this does not confine them to relaxing solely in the bedroom. A preferred amenity in all primary rooms is access to air, and inversely, heating. If the guest does have access to a lounge area, spicing it up with household plants, sectional sofas, rugs and carpets, coffee table, side tables, and the aesthetic bookshelf are top-notch attributes. Entryways or halls should have access to mirrors and a basic shoe rack. The windows should incorporate drapes. The drapes can be blackouts for the bedroom to ensure optimal sleeping conditions. Lounge and living room areas are usually the primary areas for decor, and the place where guests sit with their friends. A chic area will give the perceptions of a luxurious feel for the entire house.

Above & Beyond

Finally, as stated by Get Paid For Your Pad (2019) for the top-star experience, here is a list of amenities that can be utilized by any host:

- seasonal fruits
- cell phone with a local sim card
- bottled water
- discount vouchers and coupons of nearby stores and restaurants
- bikes, kayaks, and boats
- transport routes
- airport pickups and drop offs
- washer and dryer service in-unit

All in all, a five-star experience is largely subjective for the guest. There is an idea that spending on amenities is not necessary. However, Airbnb experiences are built around the value a host can provide to the guest. Experimenting with different amenities can open doors for increasing the listing rates and positive reviews from the guest. Essentially, supercharging your growth rate in this trade.

Inventory Checks

Many would argue the necessity of creating an inventory spreadsheet which accounts for the quantities of the amenities a host provides. However, we believe it to be an essential practice. You see, inventories generally include the set list of amenities, tools, and utensils that a host provides as an addition to the overall Airbnb accommodation experience. This is done at the expense of the host's pockets and can be considered a part of the re-investment process.

Guests might be inclined to take advantage of this luxury while not considering the effort and thoughtfulness of this approach. However, not all guests would attempt such a petty misdemeanor. Sometime there have been cases of overconsumption of particular stocks by the guests of the house. On the other hand, utensils and tools are assets of the host. In the case of extensive damage and overuse of the things could lead to deterioration, keeping an inventory checklist will allow the user to keep a basic track of the stocks. Any signs of over-consumption or damage can be reported to Airbnb or to the guest directly and seeking standard compensation would therefore take place.

House Rules and Manuals

House manuals and rules are a set of best practices intended towards the guests. These are provided by the host in accordance with the listed property. The house rules vary as every property is inherently unique. Therefore, a host is expected to go through their listings and state the necessary rules that surely apply to it. Any transgression from the original list can be used to hold the guest accountable, while anything that may have been a requirement but not listed, cannot be used if the host was not informed during the stay. Below is a list of house rules which are relevant to most houses.

Check-in time

After the booking has been made from the Airbnb platform, guests usually seek to know the exact time the house will be available to them (i.e., check-in time). The check-in time usually stands at 3 p.m. for most listings. It's built around accommodating time for cleaning and disinfection of the home. There are various means to check-in from door keypads, keys in lock boxes, self-check-in through the app, or even the case of the host physically checking the guests in. The exact method of checking in should be clearly stated in the house manual, especially in the case of self-check-ins.

Unverified individuals

The rules for an unverified individual entering or having access to the house must be specified in the house manual. Unverified guests generally mean any individual who has not been mentioned to be staying in the accommodation. There are cases when hosts might not allow any outside party to have access to the accommodation. On the other hand, many hosts allow this to its guests. The risk of allowing this lies in the liability from damage from an unverified party. In this case, the insurance policy of Airbnb will not cover the damage. Finally, in the case of a co-op listing, unverified guests can pose a security risk to the host and their family members.

Quiet hours

This rule is especially important in the case of co-op with a host or other guests. The rule outlines the hours in a day where tranquility is to be practiced by the guests. This could ensure no disturbances are endured by any other guest or by the host themselves. The quiet hours usually surround the wee hours of the night from midnight to morning.

Instructions

The house manual should account for a section that outlines the means of operating certain appliances. This is necessary when it comes to using appliances such as an outdoor grill, electric bonfires, fireplace, and so on. On the other hand, it can also include instructions of light and fan switches, how to start the heating, exhaust, and so on. Finally, instruction manuals should specify the means of accessing the boat, kayaks and any other vehicle allowed by the host.

Smoking rules

This is essential information since most listings do not allow for indoor smoking at all. In extreme cases, smoking is not allowed in the property area and vicinity, whether it be outdoors or indoors. Smoking tends to have undesirable effects on the indoor quality of air while being difficult to remove the odor before the next booking.

Wi-Fi access

Wi-Fi access, if available in the listing, should be clearly outlined for the guest. Along with the password, limit the number of users at one time, and router information if the device requires to be restarted or rebooted.

Parking rules

Parking rules should be outlined in the manual. If a designated parking spot is available for the guest, the exact parking spot, along with size and type of vehicle permitted to park, should be specified. If parking is not available, it should be specified beforehand, and guests should be requested to make their own arrangements to avoid last-minute hassles. Most importantly, guests should be advised to not block or create a hindrance for the parking spots of others. If any alternative spots are available, guests can be advised accordingly. However, liability will be the sole responsibility of the guests which in turn needs to be stated on the manual.

Security

The aspect of security is also an essential factor. It includes keeping doors locked when indoors or outdoors. Shutting windows when vacating the house, and ensuring keys are kept in the designated location specified by the host. These factors could be acknowledged as common sense; however, it still needs to be specified to ensure it remains in the minds of the guests.

Laundry

It is a common practice for hosts to request guests to leave used towels and sheets in the washer after use. The rules should specify whether the host requires the guest to start the laundry process or simply leave the used articles inside the washer.

Storage

The manual should outline details of extra amenities that might possibly be required such as toilet paper, towels, kitchen towels, plates, utensils, and so on. Finally, anything guests have stored in the refrigerator should be taken out, apart from products that have a long shelf life. A host should go forward and specify the type of food that can or cannot be brought into the house, if any. The practice could be based on the host's personal religious or lifestyle practice. Therefore, guests can be advised to not cook or consume any produce which is considered non-halal, or even to restrict from cooking meat-based meals. Usually, hosts cater a large variety of guests, and thus, allow for all categories of food in-house. However, if hosts do have special preferences, it should clearly be specified in the manual.

Directory and communication

Some hosts prefer sharing their personal contact information while others prefer to solely engage through the Airbnb messaging platform. The choice is with the host, and they can change it as per their requirements.

A collective directory of emergency numbers, grocery store details, restaurants, and tourist attractions can be listed out to further aid the guests during their travels.

Ensuring no personal items are left behind

Hosts are not responsible for any personal items that may have been mistakenly left on the premises by the guests. Usually, cleaners enter the house after the guests have departed. Therefore, it should be specified to do a final check of all belongings before locking up. Of course, the host can be informed on the case of a lost valuable. However, it holds no obligation on the host to acquire or find said valuable or compensate the guest.

Check-out and review

Finally, the checkout date needs to be clearly specified as any extra time stayed could lead the guests to be charged for one additional day. If the guests do wish to extend their stay, they can possibly contact the host. Depending on hosts availability of the rental, they can decide whether it will be possible.

Finally, the host can request for a review on the platform. Usually, the platform prompts the guest and the host after the stay is over to review each other.

The Ins and Outs

This section talked about the essential practice of preparing your property before considering listing on the Airbnb platform. The points discussed regarding ensuring repairs, childproofing, and decor are at the helm of any proper listing.

Secondly, we delved into the topic of amenities and its significance in hosting. Guest amenities are a sort of token provided by the host to incorporate a feel of luxurious and top-notch service. These services can be categorized as per the various rooms of the accommodation, and even hold the opportunity to be personalized as per guest reservations. Following this, we discussed the importance of maintaining inventory checks to ensure unnecessary consumptions, keeping stock of utensils, tools, and so on. At the end of the day, hosts are providing these at the expense of their pockets and should check whether they have been misused.

Lastly, we described the importance of creating house rules and manuals for the guest. Rules surround the best practices that every guest must adhere to while staying in the accommodation. On the other hand, house manuals are designed to aid guests in their experience with defined instructions and guidelines in accordance with the house.

CHAPTER 4
A PICTURE'S WORTH
A THOUSAND WORDS

As the chapter's namesake, in this section, we will delve into the importance of capturing photos of your listings for the Airbnb platform. Photography is essentially an art and does have its set of rules and styles which best fits different subjects. The value of stellar snaps to showcase your listings is significant. As it remains as one of the primary means a guest will choose whether they want to live at a place or not. Lack of pictures creates distrust and doubts. Whereas too many pictures may distract them from the uniqueness of the place. Thus, a balanced set of pictures which emphasizes the best parts of the house is ideal. As stated by Airbnb (2019), "Generally speaking, listings with beautiful photos receive more eyes, more interest, and more bookings, so take some time to make them shine. Draw in potential guests, highlight what's amazing, and set their expectations appropriately."

So, how do you take great pictures? What are the dimensions which are allowed by the platform? Do you use your phone, DSLR, or hire a professional? Which parts of the house should you cover? We will be covering all these and more in the first part of this section.

Platform Recommends

Airbnb platform and excerpts from seasoned hosts state the value of quality snaps of their listing and its correlation to hiring booking rates. Proper captures incorporated with editing and organization can enhance the value of each and every picture included.

The platform allows its hosts to upload a maximum of 100 photos per listing. The dimensions of the photos are not based on any stringent rules. However, according to Gunning (2020), "Airbnb recommends that hosts take pictures in a width-to-length aspect ratio of 3:2, with a minimum resolution of 1024 x 683 pixels." Just because the platform allows for a maximum upload of 100 snaps, does not mean it needs to be met till the brim. A general rule of thumb should account for 20-30 exceptional photos over an exaggerated number of blurry ones—quality over quantity any day. In terms of equipment, potential guests should not necessarily jump the gun and purchase an expensive camera. Having the skills to work one comes with practice and the science behind photography can take some time to grasp. Rather, we have phone cameras nowadays which can capture stellar pictures and conduct editing without the hassle of software or pricey gear. Basic equipment could be finding a mount or a tripod to help the phone capture stable pictures. On a final note, any outsiders who are in the pictures posted by the host should be blurred out by. Hosts should ensure to not have any images which contain anyone other than their immediate family members, or individuals who have consented to it.

Styles and Tricks

Room wise arrangements

Every room should be approached individually and captured as per its arrangement style. What this means is to prepare the rooms first as per its decor style, furniture placement and amenities. Adding personal touches to each room would spice up the decor and appearance even more. For instance, adding house plants, centerpieces on the tables, allowing for natural light and so on. The pictures are means to highlight the best parts of your rooms; therefore, an organized room is the first step.

Cleaning

It goes without saying but the room should appear spotless in the pictures. This would mean removing unnecessary objects or decor, ensuring sparkling countertops and bare floors (especially in bathrooms and kitchen). De-cluttering is also recommended as too many objects or decor pieces in one place can appear messy.

Using light

As emphasized by Airbnb (2019), "Light is a photographer's best friend. It brings out natural depth, color, and contrast in a setting. Great lighting makes your photo look more professional overall, which makes you look professional as well." A good source of lighting can be achieved utilizing the natural light of the day. Therefore, ensure blinds and drapes are pulled back to allow the natural light to pour into the room. On the other hand, a recommended way is to turn on all indoor lights to brighten up any dark spots of the area. This trick is inherently useful in capturing smaller spaces such as bathroom or storage areas. The clear view gives potential guests a much better idea of the listing.

Shooting methods

The sought-after way of capturing rooms is through the corner angle. Simply put, the technique places the room to appear in a much larger perception. The practice also incorporates the standout piece or area of the room in the focal point while capturing the picture. So, in the case of the living room, the focal point could be the lounge area. The bedroom would consist of the focus on the bed and closets. Bathrooms would contain focus on the shower area and the kitchen would focus on the countertop, stove, fridge, and basic appliances. This practice is promoted more than the standard wall focus snaps as they do not highlight the key aspects of the rooms.

Panoramic shots also can be adopted in showcasing the entirety of the premises. More so, as stated by Gunning (2020), "This type of Airbnb photo will give potential guests a better idea of the size of a space. It will also make you a more trustworthy host, as it shows you have nothing to hide." Similarly, adding some pictures of activities of your family events during holidays or parties adds color to the pictures. All in all, it showcases your lifestyle to the guests and makes them able to consider you better.

Showcasing amenities

This is also the perfect way to showcase the host's USPs of the listings. Every listing is different and always offers something great in its experience. If your listing provides access to a backyard, near a lake or a vegetative garden, play area and game room; it all can be highlighted here. It's understandable that personal advertising can seem stingy however this is a business, and it requires you to hold yourself to the highest regard by putting your best foot on the platform.

Do not hideaway from the drawbacks

While it is necessary to promote a high standard of living experience of your listing, it is also a healthy practice to show some of the possible hindrances a guest could encounter. Now, when we say this, we do not recommend going into detail about it. The practice could simply mean including a snapshot of it. For instance, a snapshot of the staircase that will be used to access the house—giving guests the idea that they need to climb up. The size of the closets, number of seating available and so on. All in all, the practice allows the guests to make additional arrangements of their own. More so, it does send away any unwanted guest who from the pictures decide the hindrances are more than they can handle—better than a bad review.

Locality

Finally, showcasing the neighborhood gives the host a further glimpse of the listing. This is especially true of the host if they are not from that state or country. While capturing the area, be sure to include the road or pathway leading up to the accommodation. Any worthwhile restaurant, historical, or cultural site.

Captions

It is also important to add captions to the pictures which are posted on the platform. Captions essentially describes the pictures and helps further organize them as per the various rooms, amenities, areas, scenic views, and neighborhood. Additionally, pictures of keypad or lock-pad locations can be shown, along with designated spots to leave keys, etc.

Organization, Layout, and Editing

Organization is a healthy practice even when it comes to posting the pictures. If as a host you upload random pictures of all your rooms without any sync with the previous pictures, it will cause confusion to the guests. Therefore, it's better to follow a system of uploading one room at a time.

Secondly, pictures which showcase the most attractive aspects of your listing should be uploaded first. This is because it will be highlighted the minute the guest clicks on your listing. After that you can ease them into the various categories in accordance with the rooms of the accommodation.

As aforementioned captions are important to give a description of the pictures. If your listing has two bedrooms, they can be uploaded individually as Bedroom one and two. Similar practice can be used for the bathrooms or any other additional rooms and storage areas.

Finally, photo editing is a recommended practice for hosts. There are many apps which, along with default camera settings of your phone, can aid the editing process. According to Gunning (2020), these are the primary editing applications:

- VSCO is a premium photo-editing app that enables users to adjust focus and clarity, use gridlines for accurate composition, and much more.
- Snapseed is Google's answer to Adobe Photoshop.
- Adobe Lightroom for mobile is one of the most popular editing apps for professional photographers.

Creating a Listing

The listing is possibly one of effective dealmakers or dealbreakers of the trade and here's why. Like the photos, listings titles and descriptions are one of the first things a potential guest will see while scrolling the app. Considering an emerging host, listing has to be a sure-fire way to attract a guest to at least click on your property. If you are a new host, you most likely will not have any reviews, therefore your landing page must be well equipped to attract people. So, what are the means for a killer listing?

The One-Liner Listing

So you have your photos, you have done your market research and set your prices. However, you are yet to see some action with your listings. It seems guests keep scrolling away without clicking at your listing and you can't seem to figure out why? Well, the answer could be because of the listing title—it's just not effective enough.

Titles are not intended to be based on any rule or system for effectiveness. Titles are completely open ended to the host and allows room for creativity and free thinking. Let us delve into this and outline some of the best practices to ensure efficacy of your titles.

Starting out, all individual listing titles are given 50 characters maximum—emphasis on characters and not words. Which means every letter is counted instead of every word (i.e., writing the title is five characters.) That does not leave a lot of legroom to work with therefore it's recommended to use all or almost all the designated characters. According to Wong (n.d.), Airbnb hosts at times use abbreviations for bathrooms (BA), with (w/), and so on to cut down on the character count. Additionally, the internal name feature allows hosts who have multiple units to further segregate their properties and include addresses there. Therefore, it does not take away from the finite characters of the listings. It is also a good idea to avoid complete caps in your titles.

Secondly, it's a best practice to avoid mundane wordings and phrases which are overused in the platform. Many hosts have been seen to use words like comfort, peaceful, beauty, open, natural, and so on. The goal is never to appear generic; it is to stand out from the rest.

Thirdly, Airbnb titles should be like a brand name. Recall how we mentioned opening an LLC gives guests credibility of the listing. Similarly, adding brand value gives your title credibility in the eyes of potential guests.

Finally, the title can be used to highlight the USPs of the listing if any. If the listing is near the beach, emphasize the surf and turf beach lifestyle. If it is around nature, focus on the holistic experience to reconnect with Mother Nature. These are examples and more can be found by browsing listings in the platform for key ideas. It is not stealing if you are just borrowing the essence.

All in all, Airbnb listings have significance. If the creativity juices are not flowing right, Floorspace (2022) recommends "try using an Airbnb title generator from *OptimizeMyBnb*. Use the titles it creates for ideas and inspiration, or copy-paste and use them as your Airbnb listing titles."

The All-Encompassing Description

Descriptors are the breakdown of your listing into easy comprehensible terms and segments. This is usually followed after the guest is notices your title and has clicked on it. If titles are to get your potential guest to click on the listing, descriptions are the means to click on the book now button. Here we share the nitty gritty of creating well rounded descriptions that speak to your guests, sell the uniqueness of your accommodations, and attract the right people.

The value of description

You must understand that a well-organized and phrased description can go a long way. However, many hosts are wary of spending too much effort on these. They might argue that guests will possibly not go through these in depth and might even outright ignore them—the data argues otherwise. According to Hospitable (2022), "Airbnb's search ranking algorithm prefers complete listings over listings that are missing things like descriptions, amenities, or house rules." Therefore, a detailed listing will rank higher across guest searches made in the platform. Adding to that Hospitable (2022) states the four categories of description summary, space, guest access and things to note, as the things successful hosts always mention.

Honesty is the best policy

As we have mentioned before, a little bit of truth about your listing can go a long way with your guest. While mentioning the truth we mean to clarify what the guest can truly expect from the stay. Also, to clarify some of the possible obstacles or troubles the guest may experience. For instance, if it's a cabin in the woods, guests should be informed that encounters with bugs are to be expected and they can pack insect spray. More so, animals can be seen, and hosts can warn customers not leave unattended food outside to attract them. Being honest allows them to make their own arrangements and thus appreciate the host looking out for them. Conversely, overselling is a big red flag to many guests.

Descriptions should be tailor made for your ideal guests

Considering the above example, a cabin in the woods experience might not be for the faint hearted. Thus, the descriptions should call out to segments of the populace who are more to the adventurous or sporty side of the spectrum. On the other hand, a listing featured in the downtown area of a bustling city can be described as the ideal place for a working adult or professional who are looking for a short and convenient stay.

Outline the unique factors

Like the title, the description is the best space to further emphasize the uniqueness of your listing. Hosts should not be shy to go the extra mile here and properly showcase their USPs while remaining honest and clear.

Tonality

Tonality of the description goes hand in hand with tailoring your descriptions as per your target audience. Thrilling and exciting tone for the buzz listings and clear and straightforward locations for the professional ones.

Descriptions should be adjusted as per timings

During seasonal times of festivals and events in your locality, descriptions can be adjusted to meet those. Usually, festive times see large influx of people and therefore represent higher potential for multiple bookings.

Brief

All in all, the descriptions should be brief. In this day and age, people do not carry the capacity to go through many circles of sentences. Instead of one large mundane paragraph, it's best to break it down into simple point-wise paragraphs which are more comprehensible and clearer. Using highlighting points and exclamations at right points also creates more focus.

The Name of The Game

This chapter concludes the section of how to prepare your property for listing on the Airbnb platform based on listings, uploading pictures of the property, and creating fantastic and detailed titles and description pages.

Pictures of the platform are one of the visual cues used by the guest to assess the worthiness of the property and whether they can consider themselves living in them. Similarly, titles are cues which attract a customer to initially consider your listings. Titles have finite character and thus hosts require creative means to state their story. Finally, the aspect of description is the trump card that motivates the guest into confirming the bookings. Descriptions should be well organized while accounting for the necessary details a potential guest needs to be aware of. The room for creativity is abundant in this portion and hosts are recommended to make the best of use of this.

CHAPTER 5
THE HONOR BADGE

A irbnb has adopted a unique feature in their platform to separate stellar hosts from the rest. This niche is a sought-after badge that many hosts strive for—known as the superhost. These categories of hosts have strived for exemplary service and have received recognition by their guests on most of their bookings. They have built their accommodations to provide luxurious service with rapid communication. They are considered to be the prime example of the surreal Airbnb experience. According to the Airbnb website, the superhost program is built around promoting and celebrating the top tier hosts who have shown credible service. According to Host Tools (2021), "Airbnb Superhosts are property owners or managers who provide an outstanding guest experience." However, the question on most emerging host's minds—what factors are relevant to becoming an Airbnb superhost?

The Qualification Process

The qualification process under the platform is strict and based on the successful completion of four factors. The performance is based on an annual period and has had to meet all the criteria within this timeline. The reviews are done every quarter of a year—any host that transgresses from the requirements can have their superhost status revoked. Here's a detailed description of them:

Hosting 10 guests

This goal is fairly straightforward and can be considered one of the lesser difficult ones of the four. Additionally, if a host does more long-term bookings, their requirements are a total of 100 days of stay broken down across three bookings. The only issue with these criteria is that it is essentially linked to the rest of the three factors.

Achieving a 4.8 or higher average rating

Ensuring the 10 guest reservations will not cut it unless you have stellar reviews across them. This makes it challenging as the host must ensure the quality of service and the value to the guest is optimal. To the point that they are considerate enough to leave positive reviews on your page. Also, they feel their stay was of quality enough to recommend the listing to their peers, family, and friends. These can be big shoes to fill initially however with regularity and competence, it can be achieved. The issue of messaging them personally to review the stay can come off as too direct. Therefore, adopting automatic messaging tools can send a prompt to the host to review.

Ensuring a 90% or higher response rate

This feature tracks the competency of hosts in getting back to guest queries on the Airbnb platform. Of course, not all queries will convert into a booking, Nevertheless a high response rate is a strong indicator of the host's performance and dedication. While this may prove to be a hassle and time consuming, there are automated alternatives hosts can adopt to free themselves. The platform allows for automated messages to be set the second a guest sends in a direct message. This ensures the high response rate and pings the host to generate a personal answer at the convenient time.

A less than 1% cancellation rate

Another difficult criterion which has to be met is to ensure no confirmed bookings are canceled. Therefore, hosts must ensure to have only a maximum of one cancellation for every 100 bookings confirmed (Host Tools, 2021). The Airbnb platform strives to ensure guests and hosts are in sync with their bookings and practices limiting cancellation on both ends. While guests have the opportunity to cancel bookings sometime even at a full or partial refund, any cancellations on the host's end could tarnish their progress towards becoming a super host. A common reason for cancellations is from double booking. Some hosts prefer to list their properties under Airbnb and other platforms offering short-term rentals, for example Booking.com. Hosts who are practicing this should ensure their calendars are synced across these websites to avoid any cancellations.

Reaping The Rewards

Though the criterion is strict, the rewards are monumentally beneficial to the superhost. A superhost will enjoy increased visibility from the platform after their promotion. Guests while browning the listing have the option to turn on "superhosts only" filter. Considering you are there; it eliminates your competition significantly. These listings have been seen to be showcased on the Airbnb newsletters which includes detailed coverage on the host and property. This proves to be a great promotion opportunity and usually feeds back to higher occupancy rates. Not only that, but certain subsidiary websites also tag along and showcase the listings on their personal platforms.

This essentially makes them unique from the rest of the competitors. A super host is more likely to garner the attention of guests. You see, trust is difficult to build initially and the superhost title is the ultimate source for guests. They value the effort put into the service and even considering paying more. The hosts could even experiment with higher rates for their listings. This may not pan out exactly like they would have wanted in local areas, however in areas of high influx of people it can be really beneficial for the host.

Lastly, industry recognition is earned via this means. Superhosts are invited to Airbnb events in their locality and even in the country. They have greater exposure to the network and chances of scaling their operations through partnerships and joint ventures. They even enjoy special benefits from the company via travel packages and year end referral bonuses.

Maintaining the Status Quo

The means of achieving the superhost title has been set out however the methods of ensuring it holds across time are tricky. Remember hosts are evaluated every three month of the year and any negligence could strip a host off this title. Therefore, certain practices must be incorporated to ensure service quality and value to guests. A step towards that direction is by creating a guest guidebook.

Your neighborhood favorite lunch spot may be the amazing sandwich store in that tiny alleyway, but it is only well-known to residents. There will be many visitors who are from outside your city, and hardly any from your area. Rarely will visitors be familiar with the neighborhood "go-to" places that you probably know like the back of your hand. After all, this is your neighborhood, and these are the locations you probably visit frequently. Good Airbnb hosts assume the position of the hotel concierge at the front desk, ready to help visitors by responding to their most frequent inquiries. Generally, guests have many queries regarding the area or locality. However, they might not feel completely comfortable asking these questions directly to the host. In the world of technology, a variety of information is available to us at our fingertips but not all may be of true value. Having a guidebook ready as a pdf folder in your listing or as a printout can greatly benefit the guests. You see, guidebooks show the hosts engagement levels and openness. A guest will be inclined to prefer hosts who strive to ensure a valuable stay for them. This can enlist a sort of positive loop of higher conversions in booking with positive feedback. This low cost and easy to do investment can be re-applied to future guests. An essential guidebook should include the following information:

- popular restaurants
- cultural centers
- museums
- walking trails and sightseeing
- nightlife activities
- public transportation options
- malls and boutique stores
- local specialties and treats

The list is not exhaustive and can be updated as per the times and developments of the area. More so, during festival or eventful periods, further sections can be incorporated to outline the historical prominence of the events, places to visit and delicacies to try. All in all, accounting for a wholesome experience.

Another popular aspect of ensuring the superhost title would be adding on the feature of cleaning service to your accommodations. Yes, there is a fee to the service, however, personally a host cannot expect to perform the same quality of service as the professionals. Accounting for the aftermath of Covid-19, guests strive a new degree of cleanliness of their stays. This involves disinfection and cleaning services that fall well beyond the reach of the host alone. The standards of hygiene pre-Covid is not the same now.

Another personalized approach involves preparing a gift package for every new guest reservation. These packages could include a handwritten note from the host directed towards the guest. More so, it can include seasonal fruits, chocolates and small gifts or trinkets. All of these are low-cost investments which are bound to be paid off via the positive loop of feedback and conversion.

Strategies for the Wallet

No doubt Airbnb is a profitable venture and the current resurgence in this field has brought about more and more individuals into this field. As stated by Meyer (2022) "There are more than 4 million Airbnb hosts, on average, an Airbnb host earns $9,600 annually, hosts have earned $110 billion as of

October 2020." So how does one protect themselves from lack of bookings or saturation in the market? How does a host ensure their profit levels are maintained and ensure costs are covered? In this section we will dive into the pricing and marketing strategies that can prove to be effective to ensure stable profits and occupancy rates across troubling times.

Pricing

Let us take a walkthrough of the Airbnb pricing structure to comprehend these strategies better:

- nightly fee
- Airbnb fee charged by the company
- cleaning fee
- security deposits
- value-added tax (VAT) and local taxes
- additional guest fee

Apart from the nightly fee set by the host, all these extra charges will be the responsibility of the guest. Any attempt to reduce any of these extra fees benefit the guest greatly and allows for price competitiveness.

Considering the above fact, offering promotions on your listings can attract new listings. This is because the rates of the Airbnb cost structures are usually applied to every listing. A potential after clicking on your listing will view a summary of the cost breakdowns. Comparing the fact that a host has offered a discount on a per night or a set night stay, will inevitably make this listing more attractive.

Similarly, a new feature on the platform 'host-only' fee structure gives room to additional savings to the guest. As stated by Floorspace (2022), "In the past, there was only a split-fee structure, where the host is charged a 3–5% host fee, and the guest is charged a 14% service fee." Using the host only fee structure absolves the guest from this fee which makes the listing greatly attractive.

Another popular method is to adjust nightly prices as per peak and off seasons. Peak seasons during times of festivities see higher demand for accommodations—increasing the rates here will be beneficial as guests will require a place to stay. Conversely, during times of low demand, attractiveness can be garnered by offering lower than normal rates.

Cancellations are common and should be expected by any host. For this to not hamper your margins, cancellation policies can be adopted. These policies range from paying a partial to a full fee, given the cancellation is close to the date of stay. Though zero cancellation fees might attract guests to consider the listing more, it is still a practice that should be maintained throughout. On the other hand, unexpected costs can arise and need immediate attention. Situations such as a leaky pipe, broken appliance, damaged furniture, can be expensive. Properly accounting for this means setting aside a fund for solely this purpose from beforehand. Thus, it will not eat away at your residual profits.

Practicing scalability is recommended for Airbnb hosts and superhosts. This practice enables you to diversify out of one unit and one geographical location. The new listing can have its own set of benefits which can be capitalized on. For instance, a beachfront listing will always attract listings. Similarly, an apartment amid a busy city will always be in demand for tourists and professionals. Purchasing or acquiring a land by the means of a rental arbitrage sounds great but could tie up your finances. As mentioned by Clark (2021) "whether you're buying a fixer-upper or a ready-to-rent vacation home, you'll still need to factor in a couple of upfront costs that could impact your initial net income." There even lies an opportunity to rent out a portion of your home through online rental platforms like Airbnb if one has a spare room. This allows you to experience a fleeting glimpse of real estate in the comfort of your own home. The process is fairly simple as it allows the owner to put up rooms for short stays at a higher rate, compared to long and binding leasing agreements. The guests will undergo screening when utilizing a platform like Airbnb and allows the owner more confidence in the people they let inside your house. Additionally, Airbnb offers insurance in the case that damages do occur. Renting a home for a long time and then re-renting it for a short time on websites like Airbnb or Vrbo is known as 'rental arbitrage.' The short-term rental market can be entered through rental arbitrage without investing in real estate. This can be both extremely profitable and difficult. The hospitality sector uses revenue per available room or RevPAR, as a metric to assess the performance of hotels. A hotel's average daily rate (ADR) is multiplied by its occupancy rate to determine the measurement.

Marketing

Property demand in the Airbnb platform is primarily based on reviews. However, there are other means to grow this further. The practices include social media presence, building a brand, optimizing with search engine optimization (SEO) tools, or even entering deals with businesses in the locality (Floorspace, 2022). Striving for exposure is a recommended path for growing popularity and higher conversion rates.

Considering the path of social media presence, there are a myriad of techniques that can be adopted. The first means would be to create a band with its own trademarked logo. This creates a persona and gives the entire venture a face or name to relate to. Incorporating your brand name and logo with Airbnb listings allows for better recognition and remembrance. Remember we are flooded with hosts of all types in this platform, differentiating yourself and your listing might actually cement yourselves in your guest's minds. Following creating a brand name and logo, we can start to consider the different social media platforms: Instagram, Meta (Facebook), and even YouTube.

Instagram

Instagram is a visual platform built around the appeal of pictures. Remember the section of effective pictures of your listings? This is where we can further utilize this. Opening a business account and posting quality pictures under the niche of traveling, lifestyle, Airbnb and so on, will pick up. The platform allows for paid promotions and marketing insight tools which can be used to tailor your content and posting. Instagram also allows for short videos known as reels. This feature can be adopted to showcase the uniqueness of the listing. Similarly, stories are video clips that are available for 24 hours on the page. Thirdly, there is the option to do a few minutes video clip under Instagram TV (IGTV) which can be utilized to showcase the historical attributes, promote seasonal events and so on. Last but not the least, we have posts which can be used to focus on specific still pictures. The practice is to ensure regular posting and adjust your strategies as per the insights to create a following.

Meta

Meta, formerly known as Facebook, has always been a massive platform for promoting business. As mentioned by IGMS (2021), "52% of travelers look for recommendations on social media when planning a trip. Surprisingly, 42% of posts on Facebook are related to travel" Similarly as Instagram, the platform allows for a business page through which posts, stories, reels, and short videos can be posted. Since the takeover of Instagram under the mantle of Meta, you can post across Instagram and Facebook via any of the platforms.

YouTube

This is more of an opportunity when scalability is involved as this could possibly require hiring professionals. A great strategy to help personalize your business is by starting a YouTube channel. The creation of videos that showcase your properties should be the main goal of your YouTube marketing plan. Create interesting information that promotes local knowledge among visitors. Create movies, for instance, that highlight the greatest sights in your region and what makes them so important to see. For tourists, your video material must be truly valuable. They will value advice and recommendations from someone who is well-versed in the area. The development of your YouTube subscriber base should be a key component of your Airbnb marketing strategy. A challenging step of increasing views and following is to share the content across multiple platforms.

The Honor Roll

This chapter concludes the aspects of the qualification process for Superhost and its benefits. It's important to remember the four factors that are essentially linked to each other when it comes to seeing progress toward the honor badge of superhost. Superhosts are evaluated regularly, once every three months to ensure they are maintaining their status quo. Thus, it is imperative hosts practice strategies such as creative informative guidebooks, personalized gifts and so on to enrich the guest experience. Higher conversion rate and positive feedback can be turned into loop feedback as per these means. Finally, we delved into the practices needed to ensure profit levels are maintained across. We further broke those strategies down as per the pricing structures and marketing strategies. All in all, these will favor the host and pay off in the future.

CHAPTER 6
MISTAKES ARE A FACT OF LIFE

I t is inevitable. Starting out in this trade you will end up making some mistakes. Starting out in any trade can be a potential and room for mistakes. The part of this process is the learning curve. How can inexperienced hosts avoid getting bad reviews on Airbnb? Being a novice host makes it easy to make several mistakes that can have a variety of negative outcomes, from your listing not appearing prominently in searches to, sometimes in more dire situations, the collapse of your Airbnb business. To assist you avoid the murky waters of Airbnb, we have put together this list of things to keep in mind. Your Airbnb business is successful if your visitors are pleased with your offerings and give you favorable reviews and a 5-star rating. To satisfy the needs of their guests, the Airbnb Superhosts put in a lot of effort and go above and beyond. Let us consider some tried and tested circumstances which experienced hosts have advised to look into.

Expectations

Over exaggeration and painting a glossy picture of our listing to attract guests, does not play out well. The reason is obvious, they are bound to find out sometime during their stay. In that moment the surge of negative reviews would start to come in and which in turn will bring about the downfall of the trade. Honesty and transparency go a long way.

Over or under enthusiasm

Moderation in all things, that has been a virtue idolized by many a wise person. In terms of communication, getting too personal can be seen as being nosy and not respectful of guest privacy. Conversely, we have outlined the drawback of being too timid and reserved on the platform. The system of Airbnb is built around engagement and communication. However this needs a healthy balance.

Set themes

While your unique decor and peculiar designs might appear to attract customers to a listing, renovations might not benefit from the same luck. This is because over the top design works attract a particular niche of the populace and even so only for a minority of the time. Investing in such interiors without any expert knowledge might put the host in a financial rut.

Fixed rates

The liberty of setting and being able to change listing rates is one of the top advantages the Airbnb platform allows to its hosts. Adjusting rates as per the feedback from the market is key for success in the platform. Any host who does not take advantage of this feature risks losing out on potential guests and potential income.

Complacency

This is a big killer in almost all businesses. Any venture should strive to adapt to the changing of the market dynamics, customer needs and industry regulations. This is especially true in the current age of technology. Considering a well sorted Airbnb host, a change could shake the roots of the business overnight. Let us take the example of Covid-19, an unseen force which halted all economic movements overnight, leading to job losses and bankruptcy in a matter of months. Similarly, Airbnb itself is considered a major disruptor of the hospitality industry. Being complacent is never the answer, practicing profit satisficing in business which is to maintain a stable flow of income is viable, yet still risky. On the other hand, an egoistic approach to business never pans out well. The customer is not always right but their issues should never go unheard.

Not automating

There are a variety of automating tools available to the host to relieve them of general burdens of answering messages, managing bookings, and maintaining a synched calendar. This hampers scalability and opportunities for growth and may lead to poor performances.

Using personal contact details

A big part of the platform is built around protecting the direct identities of both hosts and guests. The system allows for messaging and booking without sharing each other's personal contact details. While at times, hosts opt to share personal numbers, this can prove to be real hassle. Maintaining privacy is a best practice in this industry and seasoned hosts would always choose to acquire a separate number and mailing address directly linked to their LLC or brand name to keep work and personal life separate.

Never actually having used an Airbnb

It can be surprising but many individuals who are considering starting their own Airbnb business have never actually tried the system themselves. As stated by Russell (2019), "I'm a member of 9 Facebook groups to do with Airbnb, and I've asked the question several times: Have you actually stayed in an Airbnb Apartment? The number of times that people have not amazed me." Staying in an Airbnb gives you the field level experience a host so dearly needs. Any host should very likely have been a guest in some form of accommodation in their lifetime. Thus, they can identify which aspects of their stay they have liked or not.

Learning and Relearning

In this chapter, we concluded the section of the necessary do and don'ts for any host. The list provided here is not exhaustive but gives a glimpse of the standard practices to avoid. To reiterate, mistakes are not uncommon, however, striving to learn from one's mistakes should always be a virtue. Considering the leniency of the Airbnb platform, hosts should take these rules and many more which they will come across in their journey to solidify their footing as the host of their guest's dreams.

CHAPTER 7
SYSTEM AUTOMATION

The typical landlord has a rather simple job: find tenants for long, quarterly or month-to-month rent leases, arrange for necessary repairs, and collect rent at the end of every month. The shortest leases are at least a month, and they require signatures of both parties. Any delay of payment by the renter could be met by penalties and they are subject to eviction. Airbnb owners and managers must play in a different league entirely. The short-term rental scene suggests that stable income is not guaranteed and is dependent on various factors.

As we have seen so far, Airbnb owners have their hands full. From creating a winning listing, responding to queries, ensuring the property is ready for use, developing strategies for pricing, arranging cleaning, organizing amenities and many more. Considering the case of a host who has scaled his business, managing multiple properties can become quite hectic—enter automation. You see, as businesses start growing, hosts will be required to delegate and prioritize other aspects of the business more. Automation and various tools relating to bookings, guest queries, cleaning and so on, are available to free up the host's time. Let us consider looking into the varied benefits and possible drawbacks of automating segments of your Airbnb business.

Benefits

Communication

Hosts ability to respond to guest queries is considered an important metric of success. It shows dedication and availability and one of the criteria to achieve the status of superhost. Communication software is available that allows them to respond to guest queries and requests. The hosts can create unique templates with certain trigger words that will respond to questions. To take this further, certain software have integrated aspects of artificial intelligence (AI) and machine learning to be able to provide personalized responses to guest queries. Effective communication is one of the pillars for a five-star review.

Bookings and managing reservations

This factor is especially true for hosts who list their businesses on multiple platforms other than Airbnb. The issue with this practice is it sometimes leads to double bookings on the same timeline. Certain rental management software is built to process these kinds of circumstances. This software allows login from multiple accounts into one channel and the ability to control key aspects of the listing through the software platform. So, aspects of rate change, calendar sync, and responding to guests can be conducted with one program.

Delegation

The automation software also allows for team management and task delegation. Managing multiple properties requires maintenance and cleaning teams that will timely ensure your listings are ready for the guests. In order for them to be in sync with the listings and the various check-in and check-out dates, a host can include them in the software. Thus, less room for error and more efficiency across all the business activities.

Increased income opportunities

Certain pricing software is built to adjust as per market conditions and demand. These can be adopted by hosts to allow their listings to generate or capitalize on opportunities to generate higher revenue. This will be covered in the later segments.

Reviews

Certain automation tools have built in prompts to send in automated messages to guests for reviews. These are always done after their stay is over and the timing of the message can be adjusted as per the number of days after the stay is complete. Every review is critical and could be the one separating a host from qualifying to a superhost.

Remote working

Automation software brings the entire listing and guest management under one platform. Considering this stellar feature, hosts can practically work from anywhere. The same can be said for the team members.

Drawbacks

Costly

Automation comes at a cost which can be hefty depending on the type of software and subscription plan a host has considered. More so, adding additional components and accounts may drive monthly payments higher.

Training

It does require training and some time to get used too. The host might require spending time on the in-built training modules.

More so, spend time using the software to learn to use it to its full potential. If the host has other team members, they may require further training too.

Communication

The aspect of automating communication is quite an impressive aspect of such software. As aforementioned, a criterion for superhost is to maintain a 90% response rate with the guests. This feature can become practically impossible if the basic text automation feature is not activated. The simple feature is available in the Airbnb platform, while other separate apps have more advanced features that can be employed.

At the outset, there are mainly a handful of means to automate your communications. As the business takes off and hosts start interacting with more and more guests, they start to notice patterns. These questions and queries are common across most guests and thus can be applied and automated as templates.

Secondly, messages can be automated via the auto reply feature of most mailing applications. Popular applications such Microsoft Outlook or Gmail have built-in auto-reply to features. Guests can send in queries at various times of the day. Setting up an auto email reply will enable an immediate response.

Finally, using rental management software can further simplify this process across multiple listings. As stated by Zaragoza

(2021), "Software, like IGMS and Hosty, have features like a unified inbox, message templates, and triggered messaging."

While this may be a popular system to be employed for your listings, it is good to remember that not all questions or queries are the same. Some of the messages incoming from guests might bring up a question that falls outside of the threshold of the automation software. A good host will avail automation for messages but will keep track of all incoming traffic of messages. Yes, there are some additional software that can even provide personalized messaging. An example of such a software is Tobot which can be operated on all types of operating systems. The system learns guest queries and host's replies and can start providing answers which are tailored for every guest. The Airbnb platform is also working towards building a similar tool. As stated by Li (2021) "to support Airbnb's community of guests and Hosts, we have been investing heavily in developing intelligent CS solutions leveraging state-of-the-art natural language processing (NLP), machine learning (ML), and artificial intelligence (AI) technologies."

Housekeeping

Considering scenarios of multiple bookings across the week, require careful planning in terms of house cleaning and organization is necessary. This is an essential aspect of the entire trade as without decent housekeeping, your new guest will be checked into shabby and messy accommodation. Hiring cleaners becomes imperative in times of back-to-back bookings and they need to be kept updated of the schedule. The automation feature of most of the rental management software allows the hosts to streamline this feature.

Simply speaking, hosts should advise the cleaning team with a checklist in accordance with the apartments. These lists can be an addition or contain mandatory areas of the accommodation that need to be checked out by the team. A best practice for hosts using the rental software to include the cleaning team in the software and share their calendar with them. This way any updates or changes are noticed by both the teams. Adding to that, reminders can be set on the calendars which will further notify all the parties involved. Another best practice for hosts is to conduct a deep cleaning of the accommodation from time to time. This point is emphasized by Queen Bee Cleaning Services (2021) to maintain a practice of deep cleaning every six months. This ensures the furniture, floors, countertops remain clean and appear new. Lastly, bulk buying of cleaning supplies can also be automated. In doing so money can be saved and no costly last-minute runs to the stores are required.

Price

A critical part of success and a topic we have spoken about multiple times—price and various strategies in setting it. However, in this segment we will consider another segment of pricing which is intertwined with Airbnb automation software.

In the previous chapters we have discussed the various pricing strategies and essential factors of seasonality, festivities and changing market conditions which determine said strategies. However, manual adjustment of prices can only take into account so many factors at a time. In order to ensure competitive rates throughout the year end, automation can be considered in pricing. There are two fundamentals means when it comes to price automations: rule-based pricing tools and dynamic pricing tools (Host Tools, 2020).

Rule-based

This approach is based on automating your prices based on key rules that apply to your locality and area. This approach is much more personalized and is thus dependent on the hosts knowledge of demand changes of the area. It has been seen that this approach has been adopted by hosts who are managing one or a few properties.

Dynamic

Dynamic method is based on the principles of statistics, data, and aspects of machine learning to evaluate market conditions and set the prices. This approach is more reactive to market conditions and can change rates overnight. Hosts who are managing multiple properties usually take advantage of the dynamic system to set figure relevant prices across different listings.

In this aspect Airbnb platform has its own pricing automation tool, unfortunately it has been met with scrutiny and criticism from hosts. The feature is built to favor both hosts and guests. The system does not allow for a base rate, but rather a maximum and minimum rate. Additionally, the system has been criticized by hosts to undervalue the listings but at a higher occupancy rate. Strictly speaking, it is a platform that potential hosts can start off with but not consider during scaling.

There are myriad pricing automation services out there. Beyond Pricing is one such company that specializes in pricing software. The company has been around for a while and thus developed a comprehensive database of listings. The daily rates are set accounting for three factors: historical price, competitor price and real time demand. The system is a best fit for managing a large number of listings over various locations. Another example of price automation software is Host Tools. The convenient system is great for short term rentals and has advantages such as integration with Airbnb, message automation, calendar management and customer support. More so, the metrics allow for smart streamlining of pricing strategies. Finally, we have Wheelhouse which sets pricing rates based on factors of seasonality, day of the week, events, festivals and so on. More so, the system allows for three modes of price setting: conservative, aggressive, or balanced approach. Each of the tools described have their own benefits and drawbacks, along with their own subscription plans. Hosts would need to consider all these factors before making their decision.

Key Exchange

This is a step which the host needs to clearly define to guests well before they arrive at the accommodation. There are various methods of key exchanges which hosts practice. Generally, there are two primary concerns of hosts when it comes to key handover—security concerns of providing the keys to the actual guest and ensuring they are able to access the accommodation immediately after arrival. A well-executed key exchange procedure is efficient when it comes to guests acquiring keys, no time is wasted on part of the host and the exchange is not dependent on the host physically being present. Let us consider some of the means that are available to hosts based on the aforementioned factors.

Lockboxes

This is an easy and cost-effective investment option for key exchange. The process is simple, place the keys inside of a lockbox which can be opened via a particular combination. Hosts share the combination to the guests nearing the time of check-in via the Airbnb messaging platform. The location of the lockbox is clearly specified under 'how to get in' section of the house manual. This method apart from being cheap and effective, is hassle free and does not rely on anyone else. The only downside to this would be if for some reason the guest cannot unlock the lockbox, due to an incorrect code input.

Smart lock

Another tech-savvy investment would be the smart locks which can be installed on entrance doors. This feature can be considered the digital version of the lockbox— with a pin code which can be shared during check-in and can be previously programmed on the lock pad. Furthermore, hosts can set and change pins online without physically being there. This is also another convenient feature which gives full control to the host. However, these can be pricey and dependent on connectivity of the internet or Wi-Fi.

Using a third party

This method is dependent on the presence of a third party or guest's interaction with a third party who will hand over the physical key to them. While this has been the method practiced by many hosts initially, this method holds many drawbacks. In the spirit of being aware of them you can use the help of cleaners, nearby shops or businesses, neighbors or even Airbnb key management services to ensure guests receive their keys.

Cleaners who are hired for the accommodation can be tasked with the responsibility of handing over the key to the new guest. While this system sounds simple, cleaners will have to organize their schedules based on the guests arrival time. Hosts might also need to compensate them extra if they need to stay back late for this duty.

Similarly, the keys can be handed to businesses and shops operating around the listing. The shops have to be relatively close for guests to reach it. These places usually operate within business hours and hosts would have to mention this rule in the listing. Thus, putting an added stress on the guests to arrive within a certain time.

Next, giving the responsibility to the neighbors is possible but holds similar drawbacks as per the above two points. They would have to be home at the time guests arrive. Hosts will need to account for a contingency plan if guests arrive at unusual times.

Finally, hiring a third-party key exchange service would mean they would coordinate with the guest and be available to formally greet them when they arrive. This method does add to the charm of the stay but usually comes at a hefty cost to the host.

The process of key exchanges is essential and should be as seamless as possible for the guests. The house manual and the listing should indicate clear details on which procedure is being used and clearly outlined steps. Along with these steps, pictures should be attached to locate exact locations of the lock boxes or the particular location where the key can be acquired. Finally, hosts should be available via the Airbnb platform or on call if the guest does run into any trouble. The recommended means of self-check-in should be the way to go—considering its efficiency and seamlessness.

CHAPTER 8
THIRD-PARTY MANAGEMENT

A final segment of the automation process is enlisting a property manager or management company which specializes in dealing with short term rentals. The system is a method that hosts have been seen to employ for their listings. These individuals or institutions essentially will be running the business on your end while you reap the profits. Their service will come at a fee to you which can be based on the monthly incomes or a fixed rate. Regardless, in this section we will delve into the features of third-party property management, analysis on host's benefits and drawbacks in considering this option, payment structures and relevant alternatives.

Job Description

Property managers are essentially the personnel who act on your behalf for Airbnb listings. All the responsibilities a host would take on, property managers would have to undertake while keeping the host aware of the progress and decisions. As stated by Zucker (2022) "A property manager can do a wide variety of things, but their main job is to take care of the logistics of a rental property so that you don't have to."

Listings and bookings

Starting from editing the listing and tracking bookings, property managers will be looking after the Airbnb platform. They will have to ensure any necessary changes to the listings are undertaken which will attract more bookings. They are tasked to employ their expert opinions in rephrasing your description, titles and organizing your pictures to induce higher conversion rates. More so, if you are listed on other rental sites, they can be asked to look after the listings amongst all of them.

Maintenance

A large aspect of Airbnb hosting involves routine checks of the property to ensure everything is in order. Now, this step can be time consuming and stressful if a host has multiple properties spread across various geographical locations. Thus, the managers can essentially step in and work in collaboration with the host to ensure repairs and inspections are conducted.

Communication

Responding to guest queries over the Airbnb platform, handling requests during the stays and overall being in touch with the guests to ensure a smooth stay—these are responsibilities that property managers will have to take over. It is imperative that the response rate is maintained above 90% and the managers can even set up message automations on behalf of the hosts.

Organization and cleaning

Property managers also have to ensure regular and timely cleaning and disinfections are maintained in between back-to-back bookings. Property managers must ensure the accommodation is fully cleaned and ready before the new guests can check-in. Furthermore, they can have access to automate this feature and sync the calendar with the cleaning team to remove possibilities of errors.

Perks

There are numerous benefits and reasons why hosts consider hiring a property manager. The hosts who fall on the older demographic segment may prefer an actual person instead of a software component to manage their property. Here are some of the perks of hiring one:

- expert support and feedback

- automation of key aspects of the business
- freeing up time
- opportunity of higher cash flow
- higher conversion rate from booking
- reduced chance for errors and bad reviews

Limitations

Opposing the benefits are the flaws that entail the hiring of property managers. Thus, to allow for clear decision making, we have outlined a set of limitations which come with this service.

- cost intensive and possibility of hidden fees
- shared decision making could portray a lack of autonomy
- increased sense of risk
- lack of communication
- reduced facetime with guests

Cost Structure

The methods of fees charged by a property manager is dependent on various factors of property type, area and location, intensity of service, volume of managed rental and type of rentals (short term or long term). The fee structure is usually based upon a percentage commission on monthly earnings of the host or a fixed fee every month. However, the costs are not limited to just these and sometimes certain hidden fees have been paid by the host which have been shrewdly mentioned in the contract.

Considering the property type, for large and unique types of listings, property managers might consider charging rates which match the level of service required to manage it. For instance, listings which are based within a forest, near mountains and caves or even beside beaches and lakes. These are starkly different from your average Airbnbs and require special care and support to maintain operations. They might also account for the transportation fee of having to travel to these remote locations. According to Zucker (2022), "commission for short-term rental management is around 30% on average, but it can range from 10–50%. Short-term management costs are a lot more expensive than long-term rental property management, which is usually around 6–10%."

Intensity of service is based on the types of service the property managers will be responsible for. In this case, we can refer to their job descriptions (JD) which will have to be clearly defined by the host. Any extra tasks which are usually not covered in conventional JDs will have to be paid for in extra by the host.

Like service intensity, the number of rentals that are managed by the property manager will increase the amount of fee charged by them. The cost will go up even higher if the rentals are spaced separately between different locations.

Lastly, short-term rentals are usually much more difficult to manage than long-term rentals. Therefore, property managers have been seen to charge higher commission rates for these. This makes sense considering the multiple cleaning and organizations that are required for back-to-back bookings in short-term rentals.

Finding Your Dream Manager

As of now, there has not been a single platform which works on finding the optimal property manager based on the hosts requirement. Therefore, one needs to possibly spend time scouring the internet for verified websites and links that claim to offer these services. Given the buzz worthiness of Airbnb on various platforms on the internet, you can expect to find numerous websites which provide such services. However, hosts should proceed with caution and employ a vetting process.

The vetting process should be built to verify the background of the company or the individual managers. It should look into their portfolio of past work experiences and referrals from esteemed hosts. More so, it should look into their educational backgrounds along with any and all courses they have undertaken and completed which are relevant to this field.

Alternatives?

Yes, physical property managers are necessary if the host cannot be physically present at all times to look after the property. Yes, they specialize in managing properties and could possibly increase the overall revenue gain from the business. However, without proper vetting in place, they could in turn cause more harm than good. Consider the results of a a property manager who is underqualified, have poor communication skills and actually do not work well with the team and the host themselves. More so, the host may not be aware of the correct vetting process. During the search for one, hosts could possibly tie themselves up with scammy websites and companies that may inherently trick them out of their hard-earned money. So, are there any alternatives?

Of course, there are options, and it was our topic of discussion in the previous chapter—automation. Automating software has come a long way in basically providing a sense of third-party management to all your needs and more. As stated by Clifford (2020), an Airbnb that essentially manages itself by combining the essentials of bookings, messages, house manuals, check-in, check-out, team reminders, and reviews—can be achieved with a combination of automations software. However, we understand that irrespective of the technological benefits present, certain hosts might still prefer an in-person manager.

CHAPTER 9

THERE'S AN ANSWER FOR EVERYTHING

In this final section of the book, we thought it best to answer the most pressing questions a host may have. These questions may have possibly been covered within the chapters covered in this script. However, this will essentially prove to be the quick and easy go to guide or refresher for aspiring and seasoned hosts. We will be stating a list of frequently asked questions (FAQs) and providing brief answers to them.

Why open my house to strangers from the internet?

Through the means of the Airbnb platform, a potential host can list their housing for vetted and verified guests to use or share the accommodation for a short period of time. In opening your doors to them, the Airbnb platform will compensate you on a per night rate basis of which the host will decide in pricing.

Is it safe to host on Airbnb?

The platform prides itself on safe hosting and accommodation experiences in respect to the host and the guest. According to Svetec & He (2021), Airbnb has welcomed its 500 millionth guest and has a mere 1% of stays which turned out to be a bad experience. Of course, circumstances cannot be foreseen but the platform has policies in place to protect hosts liabilities through the free insurance policy known as AirCoverage.

Is it legal to host?

It is important to be aware of the local, community and state laws before participating in hosting activities. No state in the USA has barred Airbnb listing, they do, however, have rules and regulations in place that must be met by hosts.

What happens in the event of a guest getting hurt during their stay?

In this case, Airbnb will launch a formal investigation into the injury type, location, and reason for injury. If the reasons are justifiable, the platform will provide full compensation to its guests. However, if such an event does occur, hosts should be proactive in arranging for transportation of the guests first aid or medical care at the earliest.

Can hosts remove bad reviews from their listings?

No, hosts are not given that luxury to remove negative reviews which will be pegged to your listing. Reviews are the means of feedback for the guests and an opportunity for improvements for the host. One bad review is not the end of the road for a host. Usually, if the listing has positive reviews throughout and a bad review here and there, guests do not pay much heed to it.

How are payments handled?

The platform is responsible for handling all payments. They receive the relevant payment from the guest and remit the funds to the host as per the prevailing rates. Hosts and guests therefore do not have to engage in activities of payment at all.

How do I create a listing on Airbnb?

The listing process is simple and is clearly explained on the Airbnb platform. To put it simply, potential hosts must create a listing in a designated area. The listing must have a title, a description, address of the property, number of guests, nightly rate, and clear pictures of the accommodation with all its amenities and services. The object of the platform is to sell your listing and make it attractive for guests to consider staying here. Currently, there are numerous companies who help potential hosts to create winning listings.

What is a superhost?

Superhosts are a category of hosts who have attained the honor of exemplary service and quality from their listings. The qualification process for being a superhost is listed on the Airbnb website and is quite strict. This ensures that the quality of their service is maintained throughout.

Thank You!

This is a quick message of thanks that you picked my book from dozens of other books available for you to purchase.

Thank you for getting this and reading this all the way to the end.

Before you go, I'd like to ask a minute of your time to leave me a review on Amazon. As an indie author, every review (or star rating) matters as it helps our books become more visible on the platform thus in turn helps us reach and help more people.

Here are the links for your convenience:

Leave a review in:

US　　　　　**UK**　　　　　**CA**

CONCLUSION

"Nothing ventured, nothing gained." I would like to start the final chapter of this guide with this renowned saying from Geoffrey Chaucer. It is imperative to note success lies beyond the hardships, struggles and doubts of our day-to-day minds. Whereas success as an Airbnb host might be a combination of the hardship, struggles, doubts, and many, many more. So why do it? This is because being a host is quite rewarding. We have seen the flexibility of the trade, remoteness, and relevance to the current times and how the business is fundamentally scalable. These three factors alone affirm the path to success for Airbnb hosts.

This guide has been developed based on the prevailing market conditions and Airbnb's updated policies. There are numerous websites and companies who boast to provide a platform for training for new and potential hosts, however one would take this with a grain of salt. Our book serves to be a straightforward and practical guide for individuals considering this trade, seasoned hosts, and investors and even for the pleasure of reading. This book, though based on Airbnb and hosts, additionally serves as a further guide to the democratization of real estate—individuals who are both owners, renters, and even third-party managers, have delved into this trade form with success. A clear indication of preference from the industry can be felt by the grand number of subsidiary companies which have sprouted amidst Airbnb's popularity. Considering all the facts and many more verified by this book, it is safe to say that Airbnb hosting is a continuously growing platform. Thus, it is not too late to dip your toes in the wondrous trade. In the grand scheme of things, Airbnb will remain as the fundamental means of cracking open the hospitality industry for the mass populace. The art of hosting and guest management will be on the heels of the beautiful nexus of online booking and offline living, made possible by trailblazers we call hosts. During times of difficulty, it is good to recall that anything worthwhile demands effort, sacrifice and patience—hosting will test you on all these paradigms. It is always about the journey and not the destination. This is your call to action, and we are honored to be the light bearers in this journey with you.

REFERENCES

Airbnb AirCover for Hosts: What It Does and Doesn't Cover. (2022, June 14). TurnoverBnB. https://turnoverbnb.com/aircover-for-hosts-coverage/

Airbnb Descriptions 101, Including Examples. (2022, May 3). Hospitable. https://hospitable.com/airbnb-description-examples/

Airbnb Marketing Strategy: 8 Techniques to Crush Your Competitors. (2021, April 22). IGMS. https://www.igms.com/airbnb-marketing-strategy/

Airbnb Pricing Strategy: 5 Ways to Maximize Your Profits. (2022, July 28). Floorspace. https://www.getfloorspace.com/airbnb-pricing-strategy/

The Best Airbnb Pricing Tools for Small Hosts in 2021. (2020, November 13). Host Tools.

https://hosttools.com/blog/short-term-rental-tools/best-airbnb-pricing-tool/

Chang, L. (2022, March 15). *Starting an LLC for AirBnB Hosts: Is It Worth It?* Mobile Cuisine. https://mobile-cuisine.com/legal/airbnb-host-llc/

Clark, R. (2021, June 14). *Is Airbnb Profitable for Hosts? 14 Tips to Increase Airbnb Income.* Lodgify. https://www.lodgify.com/blog/increase-airbnb-income/

Clifford, R. (2020, November 23). *Hiring An Airbnb Property Manager? You NEED to Read This...* Airbnb Smart. https://airbnbsmart.com/airbnb-property-manager/¶

Fernando, J. (2022, July 31). *What is an LLC? Limited Liability Company Structure and Benefits Defined.* Investopedia. https://www.investopedia.com/terms/l/llc.asp

Folger, J. (2022, July 07). *How Airbnb Works.* Investopedia. https://www.investopedia.com/articles/personal-finance/032814/pros-and-cons-using-airbnb.asp

Griffiths, C. (2021, September 25). *How To Conduct An Airbnb Market Analysis | Expert Advice.* Lifty Life. https://www.liftylife.ca/airbnb-market-analysis/

Gunning, P. (2020, November 24). *How to Take Great Airbnb Photos: An Essential Guide for Success.* IGMS. https://www.igms.com/airbnb-photos/

Guttentag, D. D. (2016, August). *Airbnb Study.* http://www.dg-research.com/airbnb-study.html

Hospitality Industry Statistics to Have on Your Radar in 2022. (2022). Hospitality News & Business Insights by EHL. https://hospitalityinsights.ehl.edu/hospitality-industry-statistics-you-need-to-know-in-2022

How to Become a Superhost on Airbnb—and Maintain It. (2021, February 16). Host Tools. https://hosttools.com/blog/airbnb-rentals/become-airbnb-superhost/

How to Write the Best Airbnb Listing Titles (with Examples). (2022, July 5). Floorspace. https://www.getfloorspace.com/best-airbnb-titles-examples/

Kaushik, S. (2021, September 17). *AirDNA Review: Does It Still Hold Up in 2022?* Airbtics. https://airbtics.com/airdna-review/

Kaushik, S. (2021, September 19). *Mashvisor Review: Still Useful in 2021?* Airbtics. https://airbtics.com/mashvisor-review-still-useful-in-2021/

Li, G. (2021, August 10). *Task-Oriented Conversational AI in Airbnb Customer Support.* Medium. https://medium.com/airbnb-engineering/task-oriented-conversational-ai-in-airbnb-customer-support-5ebf49169eaa

Meyer, S. (2022, July 7). *Airbnb Statistics and Host Insights [2022].* The Zebra. https://www.thezebra.com/resources/home/airbnb-statistics/

Responsible Hosting in the United States. (n.d.). Airbnb. https://www.airbnb.com/help/article/1376/responsible-hosting-in-the-united-states

Riddles, C. (2021, October 29). *12 Steps To A Profitable Airbnb Pricing Strategy.* IGMS. https://www.igms.com/airbnb-pricing/#1_Consider_Your_Property_Location

Russell, T. (2019, November 23). *21 Common Mistakes Airbnb Hosts Make.* Short Rental Pro. https://www.shortrentalpro.com/21-common-mistakes-airbnb-hosts-make/

Serrano, L., Sianes, A., & Ariza, A. (2020, December 16). *Understanding the Implementation of Airbnb in Urban Contexts: Towards a Categorization of European Cities.* MDPI. https://www.mdpi.com/2073-445X/9/12/522

6 Strategies on How You Can Automate Airbnb Cleaning. (2021, December 17). Queen Bee Cleaning. https://www.qbclean.com/blog/6-strategies-on-how-you-can-automate-airbnb-cleaning/

63 Amazing Ideas to Make Your Home Airbnb Ready. (2019, October 21). Get Paid For Your Pad. https://getpaidforyourpad.com/blog/make-airbnb-space-guest-ready/

Svetec, J., & He, S. (2021, May 12). *Common Questions That Potential Airbnb Hosts May Have.* Dummies. https://www.dummies.com/article/home-auto-hobbies/travel/common-questions-that-potential-airbnb-hosts-may-have-271282/

Top 5 Photo Tips for a Stellar Listing. (2019, June 19). The Airbnb Blog. https://blog.atairbnb.com/top-5-photo-tips-for-a-stellar-listing/

Ward, C. (2019, July 30). *How to Prepare Your Home for Airbnb: Tips to Rent Out Your Home.* Good Housekeeping. https://www.goodhousekeeping.com/uk/house-and-home/a28539435/renting-home-airbnb/

Why Do People Stay in Airbnb? (n.d.). EHL Insights. https://hospitalityinsights.ehl.edu/travelers-airbnb-study

Wong, A. (n.d.). *How to Write Airbnb Titles to Increase Bookings.* Hosthub. https://www.hosthub.com/blog/how-to-write-airbnb-titles-to-increase-bookings

Zaragoza, R. (2021, November 17). *The Complete Guide to Airbnb Automation.* Mashvisor. https://www.mashvisor.com/blog/airbnb-automation/

Zaragoza, R. (2021, November 26). *Airbnb Rental Market Analysis: A 7-Step Guide.* Mashvisor. https://www.mashvisor.com/blog/airbnb-rental-market/

Zucker, C. (2022, March 10). *Should I Hire a Property Manager? Pros & Cons for Airbnb Hosts.* TurnoverBnB. https://turnoverbnb.com/hire-a-property-manager/

Printed in Great Britain
by Amazon

24570864R00079